Perfect Homemade
151+ Recipes
Linda Huerta and Sarah Roberts

© 2013

All Rights Reserved. No part of this publication may be reproduced in any form or by any means, including scanning, photocopying, or otherwise without prior written permission of the copyright holder.

Disclaimer and Terms of Use: The Author and Publisher has strived to be as accurate and complete as possible in the creation of this book, notwithstanding the fact that they do not warrant or represent at any time that the contents within are accurate due to the rapidly changing nature of the Information Age. While all attempts have been made to verify information provided in this publication, the Author and Publisher assumes no responsibility for errors, omissions, or contrary interpretation of the subject matter herein. Any perceived slights of specific persons, peoples, or organizations are unintentional. In practical advice books, like anything else in life, there are no guarantees.

First Printing, 2012

Printed in the United States of America

Contents

Introduction
Why Should You Make Your Own Baby Food
    Additives
    Pesticides
    Economics
    Healthy Diet
    Salt
    Environmental Issues
    Allergic Reactions
    Whole Milk
    Mixing Food - When is Your Baby Ready?
    Constipation
    Brain Development
    Supplies Needed
    Blenders vs. Food Processors
Storing Homemade Food
    Refrigeration
    Freezing
Nutrient-Rich Foods
    Flax seed
    Pumpkin Seeds
    Sesame Seeds
    Protein
    Potassium
    Carotenoids
    Beta Carotene
    Vitamin A
    Vitamin C
    Calcium

Helpful Hints for Cooking
- Vegetables
- Seasoning
- Onions and Garlic
- Meats
- Using Formula or Breast Milk

Squash
- Butternut or Acorn Squash Puree
- Baked Apple and Acorn Squash
- Baked Squash Bowls
- Butternut Squash and Potato Puree
- Stuffed Squash
- Cinnamon Squash Puree
- Carrot, Butternut, and Leek Puree
- Butternut Squash and Cauliflower Puree

Smoothies
- Banana Ginger Smoothie
- Pumpkin, Apple, and Banana Surprise
- Pumpkin and Banana Smoothie
- Pina-Coco-Ba Smoothie
- Bananarama
- Raz-a-Taz
- Peach Foamy
- Pineapple Delight
- Watermelon Smoothie
- Banana Raspberry Smoothie
- Mango Smoothie

Dips
- Guacamole (After one year)
- Cucumber Yogurt Dip

- Bean Dip
- Hummus
- Strawberry and Peach Fruit Dip
- Creamy Lemon Dip
- Cream Cheese Dip
- Cottage Cheese Dip

Avocado
- Avocado Rolls (Recommended for 2 years old and above)
- Avocado and Cream Cheese Spread
- Avocado Fruit Salad
- Avocado Mango Spread
- Avocados and Peaches
- Avocados and Pears
- Avocado, Cucumber, Tomato, and Cheese Salad (Over 1 year old)

Bananas
- Bananas Foster
- Bananas and Pumpkin
- Banana and Avocado Mix
- Hot Bananas

Pumpkin
- Pumpkin Puree
- Pumpkin and Apple Puree
- Peach and Pumpkin Puree
- Pumpkin Puree with Pizzazz
- Baked Pumpkin Slices
- Pumpkin, Peach, and Avocado
- Pumpkin and Yogurt Puree

Sweet Potatoes

Sweet Potato Puree
- Scalloped Sweet Potatoes

- Sweet Potato Apple Mash
- Sweet Potatoes and Squash
- Peachy Yam Bake
- Roasted Sweet Potatoes

Peas
- Creamed Peas
- Peas with Mint and Rice
- Zesty Peas, Cauliflower, and Tofu
- Peas and Pasta Shells with Parmesan
- Spanish Rice with Peas

Breakfast
- Brown Rice Cereal
- Apple, Pumpkin, and Oatmeal Breakfast Baby Food Recipe
- Blueberry Muffins (Over 1 year Old)
- Oatmeal with Apricots (9 months)
- Cheesy Eggs and Ham (9 months)
- Chile Quiles (Over one year old)
- French toast Dippers (Over one year)
- Roast Beef Hash
- Crushed Cheerios in Banana Puree
- Eggs with Tomatoes and Cheese
- Sausage, Egg, and Cheese
- Orange Zucchini Muffins (12 months)
- Sweet Potato Pancakes

Chicken
- Chicken, Rice, and Applesauce
- Mixed Chicken and Vegetables
- Creamed Peas and Chicken
- Chicken with Blueberry Sauce and Mint
- Breaded Chicken

    Rice and Chicken
    Carrots and Turkey
    Chicken, Potato, Cheese, and Rice
    Turkey Chili

Soup
    Mama's Special Soup (Over one year)
    Sweet Potato Soup
    Squash and Rice Soup
    Sweet Potato Soup (8 months)
    Lemony Chicken and Rice Soup
    Cold Vegetable Soup
    Cream of Pumpkin Soup
    Squash Soup (8 months)

Apples
    Applesauce
    Apple Zing Puree
    Apples and Yogurt
    Pear and Apple Puree
    Apple Grahams Delight
    Sweet Cinnamon Apples

Rice
    Rice with Apple and Butternut Squash
    Rice Pilaf
    Spanish Rice
    Fried Rice
    Cheesy Rice with Bacon Bits
    Cheesy Rice with Lemon
    Pumpkin Risotto (8 Months)
    Roast Pumpkin Risotto
    Sweet Potato Risotto (Over one year)

- Fruit Dishes
  - Roasted Pears (Over one year)
  - Papaya
  - Tasty Peaches
  - Peach Puree
  - Papaya Puree
  - Kiwi Puree (8 months)
  - Kiwi and Banana Surprise
  - Mango Puree (6 months)
  - Mango and Banana Puree
  - Banana and Papaya Puree
  - Melon
  - Strawberries and Creamy Yogurt
  - Banana and Tofu
  - Strawberry Nectarine Puree
  - Apple Cinnamon Prunes
- Other Vegetables
  - Healthy Green Beans
  - Cauliflower Puree (6 months)
  - Breaded Cauliflower
  - Broccoli Puree (6 months)
  - Sautéed Broccoli Puree
  - Sautéed Broccoli
  - Potato and Zucchini
  - Roasted Carrots
  - Zucchini Puree
  - Broccoli with Cheese Sauce
  - Parmesan Asparagus Puree
  - Mixed Vegetables
- Pasta

- Pasta and Carrots
- Lasagna Baby
- Baby Pasta and Meat Sauce (Over one year old)
- Baby Fettuccini
- Pasta with Tomatoes and Broccoli
- Pasta with Zucchini

Fish
- Grilled Salmon
- Cream of Cod
- Cod Casserole
- Salmon with Dill
- Tomato and Basil Cod
- Baked Fish with Sweet Potato
- Carrot Fish
- Fish Sticks

Pork
- Creamed Peas and Pork
- Pork, Green Beans, and Potatoes
- Pork and Sweet Potato
- Red Pepper Pork with Rice
- Pork in Apricot Sauce
- Pork Casserole
- Maui Pork

Beef
- Hearty Beef Stew
- Creamed Peas and Beef
- Beef with Carrots and Potatoes
- Yummy Meat Sauce
- Meatballs
- Meat Loaf (Over one year)

- Baked Beans
- Potatoes
  - White Potato Puree
  - Roasted Red Potatoes
  - Mashed Potatoes with Spinach
  - Potatoes and Cauliflower
  - Scalloped Potatoes
- Cheese
  - Cheesy Baked Potato
  - Mac 'n Cheese
  - Shells with Parmesan and Butter
  - Cottage Cheese with Peaches
  - Sliced Cheese and Grapes
  - Cheesy Quesadillas

Introduction

Welcome! As a parent, you're here because you're interested in the overall well-being of your infant or toddler, which is of the utmost importance. As a parent myself, I understand that there are so many issues to be concerned about, many of which you have no control over. From the moment my first child was born, I wanted the best start. I breast fed and I read all the parenting and nutritional material I could get my hands on. Each day, I strove to offer my son the best of everything.

It has been an immense deal of fun putting together the information for this book, rich in memories of my little ones as I look back on the various stages of their lives. Such memories bring happiness to each day. My intent of this book is to help parents with the nutritional material and recipes that help to offer the best start as they begin their journey with their children. The time goes so quickly and the beginning years are some of the most adored!

I hope you enjoy the information and recipes, and even the bit of reminiscing when my children were in their baby stages. It is such a fantastic time and as one parent to another, these are days that you'll look back on and cherish for the rest of your life.

In recent years, a great deal of information has been published on infant health and well-being. A great deal of this information focuses specifically on infant and toddler nutrition. Living in this fast-paced society with technical advances and modern conveniences brings both a lot of good and evil to parents and families. The good includes medical advances, which can save people's lives. The evil includes mass- produced everyday items, including groceries and food. Again, while having this abundance of products makes shopping tremendously convenient, the downside is that we're not always aware of the fats, preservatives, dyes, and toxins found in the food we eat. This becomes of even greater importance as we consider the nutritional habits of our infants and toddlers.

As newborns transform to infants, who then transition to eating solid food, parents are faced with decisions about when to introduce solid foods and what foods to introduce. This issue becomes even more complicated if someone in the family has a history of food allergies or other health issues that can pass genetically from parent to child. Many childcare specialists even disagree on the timing of introducing solids into your baby's diet. While some say that this is not necessary until the first year of life, others say to begin this process when your baby starts to show an interest in eating regular food.

While there are a number of baby food products on the market, the current trend is toward homemade baby food, as this is a way to ensure that fresh organic products are used in the preparation of your baby's food, as well as a way for parents to save a large amount of money often spent on individual jars of food. Making baby food is actually a very simple process that involves the use of a food processor or blender to puree the different food items, including fish, poultry, vegetables, and fruits.

This book provides a discussion about this new trend of making your own baby food and will answer many common questions related to making your own baby food. In addition, we'll provide dozens of delicious recipes that you can use to prepare your baby's food.

I know these years are special and I hope that this book provides not only information and recipes you need to help build your baby's foundation, but also memories that warms the heart.

Why Should You Make Your Own Baby Food

As more people become more aware and conscientious about their diets and what they eat, more parents are turning to making their own baby food. In general, people are trying to eat leaner meats, increase intake of fruits and vegetables, and decrease consumption of fatty fried foods. As parents, before our children are even born, we make plans for their nutritional start with the question of whether to breast feed or bottle feed. This becomes challenging when you find fast food restaurants located on every corner in your city. Sometimes, just the smell of a burger grilling is enough to get you to pull over and order a big combo meal. However, if your infant gets used to eating junk food, he may become resistant to eating the healthy foods that his body needs for proper bone, muscle, and brain development.

Training your infant to eat healthy is a great way to help him start his life. Preparing the food yourself is an additional bonus that ensures higher quality and freshness to the food. As the old saying goes, "When Momma's happy, everyone's happy," and you'll quickly find that when you're able to offer homemade baby food, both Momma and baby are happy!

I wouldn't trade these years for anything - they are truly special times. The beginning stages of your baby's life is when you get to know your baby, when you begin to fill them with love, and build their foundation that helps to ensure their future.

There are many reasons in favor of preparing your own baby food at home. The first and foremost is that it increases your confidence that the food you're giving your infant is fresh, healthy, and free of unnecessary preservatives, dyes, pesticides, and toxins. Other reasons in favor of making your own baby food include cost effectiveness, avoiding or controlling the amounts of salt and sugar in your baby's diet, and the fact that it is environmentally sound. Finally, if your baby is allergic to any food, making your own baby food will reduce the risk of some hidden allergen/s in your baby's food, which could cause a severe allergic reaction. Let's take a closer look at some of the issues listed here.

Additives

In order for baby food to be processed, packaged, and kept on a shelf for any period of time before it is sold, it must have some preservatives to keep it from going bad. Common preservatives used in preparing pre-packaged food include, Sodium Nitrate, Hydrogenated Vegetable Oil, Monosodium Glutamate (MSG), Olestra, and artificial coloring that includes any ingredient that starts with FD and C. Such foods often contain artificial sweeteners, the most common being high fructose corn syrup, aspartame, dextrose, and saccharin. Monosodium glutamate (MSG) is another preservative often found in frozen or processed foods. Some people sensitive to MSG experience severe side effects when they ingest this with their food. These side effects include numbness, mood changes, nausea, and headaches. Chinese food has been the type of food most often associated with MSG additive. If you take your infant to a Chinese food restaurant, be sure to request that the food you order is prepared without MSG. With my little ones (I recommend this to all parents), I always brought the baby's food with us to the restaurant. This is a big advantage, as you don't have the concern of unhealthy ingredients nor do you get your baby or toddler off track.

As you make your own baby food, you'll notice that many recipes, especially those for rice or risotto, call for chicken stock or bouillon. It's worth the effort to make your own bouillon or at the very least to try to buy stock low in additives and preservatives, especially salt. Finally, artificial colorings are often used to enhance the presentation of foods, such as meat and are frequently used in junk food, such as cookies, candy, and cake. Whenever you see FD and C on the label, this indicates that some type of dye has been used in this food.

These unnatural elements are difficult for any healthy human body to digest and are much more difficult for your infant, who has a sensitive stomach. Our babies are delicate and the pain a parent feels when their child has an upset stomach is heart wrenching. My youngest had such a sensitive system that one wrong feeding resulted in hours of screaming, burping, and uncomfortable pain.

Pesticides

Pesticide contamination of food is one of the biggest concerns when 1 your infant. Much of the produce used today to make baby food has been exposed to pesticides. Thus, unless you're buying organic products, it's likely that your fresh fruits and vegetables have been exposed to pesticides. However, it is important to note that some fruits and vegetables, mainly those with thin skins and/or no peels at all, are more susceptible to absorbing pesticides than those which have thicker skins. You may also want to consider that organic foods tend to be more costly than regular fruits, vegetables, and meats.

Fruits and vegetables, which are included in the list of foods with higher risk of absorption of pesticides include potatoes, winter squash, grapes, cucumbers, pears, strawberries, green peppers, red peppers, spinach, lettuce, cherries, peach, nectarines, blue berries, green beans, apples, and apricots. As stated before, most of these foods have thin skins or possibly no skin at all, which is what makes them more likely to absorb any pesticides that they have been exposed to in the growing process.

Pesticides are stored in body fat. The human brain is composed mostly of body fat, which makes it a natural place for these pesticides to settle. Infants are also susceptible, as their bodies have a great deal of baby fat, such that pesticides are likely to remain in their system. Many of these pesticides have been linked to medical disorders, such as weakened immune systems, cancer, or Attention Deficit Hyperactivity Disorder. This is one reason that I started both an indoor and outdoor vegetable and fruit garden.

The fruits and vegetables with lower risk of pesticide contamination include sweet potatoes, cantaloupe, broccoli, watermelon, avocado, sweet corn, onions, cabbage, cauliflower, Brussels sprouts, eggplant, mangoes, grape fruits, bananas, and kiwi. For these foods, you're probably safe with purchasing non-organic products, as their thick skins serve as a natural barrier to the pesticide. However, if you're still concerned, regardless of the skin's thickness, by all means proceed with purchasing or growing all organic fruits and vegetables.

On a side note, an outing to your local farmer's market can be great fun for a parent and child, as it allows for opportunities to see and sometimes taste all sorts of fruits and vegetables. Your infant will be fascinated by all of the colors, smells, and shapes of the various items for sale. This activity can serve to kill two birds with one stone, as you're spending some bonding time with your infant, while at the same time purchasing some of the freshest, highest quality produce on the market. Both of these activities provide long term positive benefits for your infant. When you build a healthy nutritional foundation with plenty of fruits included, you have a lot to look forward to. My son, who is no longer a baby, grabs fruit from the fruit bowl for his snacks. As a mom, it's a wonderful feeling to see your child eat peaches and oranges on their own and by introducing the fruits now, in a tasty manner; you can help to ensure this.

Economics

With inflation rising and families feeling stressed by increased costs for everyday goods, the average family is looking to save money wherever they can. With your young infant, you have probably noticed the increased costs related to formula, diapers, baby clothes, toys, and other infant products. As you transition into using baby food (especially if you opt to use processed store-bought food), you'll incur the additional cost of purchasing these items.

It is estimated that families spend on average anywhere from $50 to $300 per month on baby food. This added cost will take a chunk out of your monthly budget, on top of any money that you're already spending on groceries for the rest of your family. These additional costs are one of the biggest reasons that people opt to make their own baby food. You will save both money and time by not purchasing individual jars of food, as well as saving gas, time, and money on constant trips to the store to purchase food. As your baby grows older and is able to eat a greater variety of foods, you'll even be able to make his food out of ingredients from your own dinner.

Healthy Diet

While some baby fat is "just part of the baby" and cute, weight gain and obesity are very serious public health issues that impact a large number of people both young and old, all over the world. As parents, we strive to take all measures to build a healthy nutritional foundation for our babies and avoid food that contributes to obesity and illness. Increased numbers of children are diagnosed with serious medical conditions, such as Type 2 diabetes and high blood pressure at a very young age. These children may go on to experience severe weight problems throughout elementary school, middle school, and high school. As a result, they are likely to be teased by their peers due to their size, as well as alienated from some peer groups within the school and the community.

The food that you feed your young infant is likely to set the foundation for future taste and dietary choices. If your child's food is high in sugar content, your child will become accustomed to a sugary flavoring and may opt to eat more sugary foods when given the opportunity to choose. As you purchase products at the store, pay close attention to ingredient labels, as these will help you to spot hidden and added sugars. Sugar is often presented with different names, including corn syrup, evaporated cane juice, dextrose, and sucrose.

Other artificial sweeteners, which are commonly found in food products, include Aspartame, NutraSweet, and Equal, Sweet 'N Low, Saccharin, and Splenda are common. Increased levels of sugar in everyday foods have resulted in higher obesity rates, especially amongst children. Some of these sweeteners are known to cause damage to both the brain and the nervous system. Again, this supports your choice for making your own baby food so that you ensure that none of these ingredients is added to your baby's food. You'll find that when sugar is included in a recipe in this book, it is typically brown sugar.

In the past few years, trans fats have become a big topic within the restaurant and food industry. Fast food restaurants have taken a hard hit with claims that state they contribute to the worldwide obesity problem. This is because the products they market for kids are often very high in trans fat. The reason for using these fats is due to the fact that they're made up of hydrogenated liquid unsaturated fats, which are more solid and allow a longer shelf life.

Take five minutes to read the labels on the food in your shopping cart and you'll be amazed to see how many have hidden trans fats. The biggest offender, yet one that is least suspected is found in salad dressings. Other foods, such as potato chips, cookies, and margarine also have high levels of trans fats. While you probably won't be able to prevent your kids from eating foods with trans fat, you can limit their consumption by paying attention to product labels and avoiding fast food eateries.

When your children have a healthy foundation, they want to eat healthy. Preparing your own baby food will also help you to control the amount of fat within your baby's diet. In our home, "goodies" have been replaced with frozen yogurt drops, healthy crackers, and bran muffins and so on. I love to access the "Mommy food blogs" to find delicious, healthy recipes that the kids will love.

Salt

Processed, frozen, and canned foods are often loaded with salt, one of the most popular ingredients used for preserving foods. Consuming high levels of salt in your diet can lead to heart disease and high blood pressure. The best way to reduce the salt present in your child's diet is to avoid processed and canned foods. Making your own baby food will help you to accomplish this goal.

Salt is always an option that can be excluded from the recipes in this book. Overall, by doing this, you'll have much more control over your infant's diet and health. As a parent, when you model healthy eating habits and make healthy choices, your child is more likely to follow in your footsteps. As a kid, I remember my brother would make a pile of salt when eating French fries and I quickly began doing the same, thinking that was the "true" way to enjoy French fries. Today, there is plenty of information available so we can offer our children a healthier foundation.

Environmental Issues

As a society, we have become accustomed to the convenience of using individualized packages and bottles for foods and beverages that we eat and drink. Processed baby food is a prime example of this. Depending on the age, size, and appetite of your infant, each jar of baby food may only be used for one or two feedings. Being that your baby will eat at least three meals a day, seven days per week, this could result in you using anywhere from fifteen to twenty jars per week! That's a lot of glass, which may or may not get recycled, depending on your own habits. Therefore, by making your own baby food, you're eliminating a large number of jars that are thrown away or need to be recycled. Reducing waste is important for maintaining a healthy environment.

Allergic Reactions

Finally, avoiding potential allergic reactions is a strong reason for making your baby's food. If you use fresh and organic ingredients, you know exactly what is in your baby's food. No hidden additives or colorings, which might be bad for your baby's health.

If your baby does show some type of reaction after eating homemade baby food, it's easier to pinpoint what caused the allergic reaction so that you can avoid the use of that food to determine if the allergy symptoms go away. Each time I introduced a new food to my children, I would wait four or five days before I introduced another. This allows you time to determine whether the baby suffers from allergic reactions or digestive problems with the food.

While you can start to introduce solids at four months of age, many doctors recommend waiting until six months of age. By six months, baby's immune system has matured to the point that he is more likely to exhibit signs of allergic reactions. For infants under six months of age, it can take up to a week for allergy symptoms to show, which is why it is recommended that you introduce one food and wait four or five days prior to introducing other foods.

Also, for babies under one year of age, certain foods are not recommended due to their high potential for triggering a food allergy. These foods include egg whites, wheat, berries, honey, peanuts, nut products, acidic fruits, and shellfish. Some leafy green vegetables, such as spinach, collard greens, and turnip greens are also on the wait list to be used after baby's first birthday. At one year, you can introduce eggs, beef, fish, pasta, graham crackers, wheat cereal, honey, all fruits and vegetables, and whole milk. At this point in time, the main thing to be aware of are foods that can choke your baby. Ensure that foods are served in a size that your baby can easily swallow.

Honey can be introduced at one year. The reason that it is avoided for so long is that honey can contain spores, which can cause botulism in infants. Strawberries, tomatoes, and other acidic citrus fruits can also be introduced at baby's first birthday. At age two, you can introduce all nuts, raisins, popcorn, raw vegetables, and peanut butter.

As stated earlier, for infants under one year old, it is not recommended to offer wheat products. This is due to the high incidents of gluten allergies, which are being reported among both kids and adults today. Gluten is a protein found in a number of grains, such as wheat, barley, and rye. Grains that do not have gluten include rice, Quinoa, and millet.

Allergic reactions to gluten can range from mild discomfort in the stomach to full blow anaphylactic shock. In order to reduce the potential for your infant having a gluten allergy, it's important to hold off on giving your child wheat products until their first birthday.

Once you do introduce wheat, barley, or rye products, pay attention for any behavioral changes or rashes which may represent an allergic reaction. If you think that your child is allergic to gluten, please discuss this with your pediatrician, as he or she may require an allergy test or referral to a nutritionist for assistance with meal planning.

Whole Milk

As you switch your baby over to whole milk, you may experience some resistance, as she needs time to get used to this new flavor. I had mixed reactions with mine. If your baby was previously drinking formula, you can mix one part formula with one part milk and each day reduce the amount of formula until your baby is drinking only milk.

You can also try mixing one part yogurt milk with one part milk and then each day reduce the yogurt milk until she is drinking just the regular milk. Yogurt milk is sweeter to the taste and is a good transition to regular milk. Other alternatives to milk include rice, soy, or almond milk. Your baby needs to have two to three servings of calcium-rich food per day. This is also a good time to introduce water served in a Sippy cup with meals.

Mixing Food - When is Your Baby Ready?

There are some tell-tale signs to help you to know when your baby is ready to start eating solids. First and foremost, he will be very interested in the food that you eat. He might even try to reach out and grab your food or babble, which indicates that he wants what you're eating.

In order to eat solids, your baby must first be able to do a couple of things. He must be able to sit up in his high chair independently. Second, he should no longer display the natural tongue reflex, which causes him to stick out his tongue when anything is put in his mouth. If you try to feed your baby food and he completely shuns it or pushes it away, this might be too soon. Give it some more time.

Some of the first solids that you can start your baby on will be rice cereal, apple sauce, pear, sweet potatoes, and carrots. This is an exciting time and you'll find that you laugh and cry in frustration if you have a picky eater. My second child was such a picky eater that I thought we'd be on rice cereal forever. The high chair became a time when I wouldn't know what to expect. As a mom, I wanted every nutrient in my child. The key here is to not be discouraged and to continue introducing foods. As a mom of experience, I can honestly say that it can be a tough stage, but it definitely is a stage that begins a new cycle of development for your baby. You want the best for your baby so don't give up! I hear so many moms say, "Oh, my baby will only eat sweet potatoes…"

This is definitely not the key to a solid, healthy foundation.

Constipation

Constipation can occur once you start solid foods such as bananas. Rice cereal is especially constipating for babies. Pureed prunes, peaches, or diluted prune juice helps constipated babies so start with prunes and peaches prior to other foods, such as apples, bananas carrots, corn, dairy products, nuts, rice, white bread, and white potatoes.

Relieve constipation with apricots, citrus, flax oil, grapes, green veggies, peaches, plums, prunes, raisins, salad, whole grain bran cereals, and whole grain breads. Probiotic liquids or powders also help regulate the digestive system.

I suggest using a quarter (¼) cup of aloe juice daily for babies over six months. You may also use mineral oils or magnesium supplements of 200 milligrams daily to help your baby digest (always get your pediatrician's advice first!).

My oldest child experienced some constipation, but after I began to introduce foods to help with constipation, the wrinkled faces and frustrated looks suddenly disappeared. Constipation is uncomfortable for babies and something that you should help to eliminate through diet.

Brain Development

In the first five years of life, your baby's brain is growing rapidly, such that it reaches 90 percent of its adult size by age five. Of all the human organs, the brain is the one most impacted by nutrition. For infants and toddlers, about 60 percent of their nutritional energy is used for brain development and twenty-five percent of school age children's nutritional energy goes into brain growth. Bearing this in mind, you can see the importance of eating foods that offer benefits toward brain development and avoiding those that may actually cause damage to the brain. One way to look at this is to think about foods as being Smart foods and Dumb foods.

Over the years, most people have heard about the benefits of eating fish because fish is highly enriched with Omega-3 fatty acids. Thus, fish, especially salmon, has always been considered a Smart Food. Walnuts are another great source of Omega-3s. You can start to introduce walnuts to your toddler after age one. A great way to introduce walnuts is by preparing a nutty butter that can be spread on bagels, bread, or crackers. Remember that peanut butter should not be introduced until age two due to the potential for allergic reactions.

Another Smart Food that has gained recent popularity is blueberries since they're enriched with nutrients that serve as powerful anti-oxidants. Blueberries have a great impact on the blood-brain barrier, which filters out unhealthy substances and seals in healthy substances for the brain. In addition, blueberries have an impact on the functioning of neuro-transmitters that actually speed up the signals sent by the brain. Green leafy vegetables such as spinach, collard greens, asparagus, and bok choy contain properties similar to those found in blueberries.

Dumb foods include those which are high in trans-fat, have high sugar content with low protein, those which are pre-processed, and those which contain additives. These foods basically have no nutritional value at all, such that eating them essentially equates to filling your body with junk. Chemical additives have been shown to have a negative affect the mitochondria, which acts like a battery for your brain. The excite-toxins found in these dumb foods throw off the natural balance of neuro-transmitter activity in your brain. Some examples of dumb foods are aspartame, hydrogenated oils, and monosodium glutamate.

Carbohydrates are the other nutritional subject talked about quite often and these days, you'll find so many no-carb and low carb diets that carbs may seem like your ultimate enemy. However, smart carbs are vital for healthy brain function. Smart carbs include foods, such as fruits, vegetables, and whole grains. These foods are made up of both protein and fiber, which helps to slow the transmission of sugar to the brain. On the other hand, bad carbs, which are found in pre-sweetened beverages and mass produced packaged foods, don't have these essential proteins and fibers so that the sugar in these foods rushes to the brain, which can cause hyperactivity and excitement. Growing up in my home, we were fast food and packaged food eaters. Pizza night was once a week, hamburgers and fries were another, and TV dinners were a regular. While the girls in the family developed a healthy diet later in life, my brother (who is still single!) has yet to. I'll visit him, only to find the fast food containers, a fridge filled with soda and foods high in carbs and stuffed with additives, and to no surprise, an overweight brother. While we all love him, he consumes an unhealthy diet that should be avoided from the beginning stages of life.

Even though you may be discontinuing use of formula or cutting back on breast feeding at the reading of this book, please note that milk is still an essential requirement for your baby's diet. Babies require at least 800 milligrams of calcium per day to help the development of their bones and brain. Calcium can be found in milk, some green leafy vegetables, and in certain calcium-fortified cereals.

Supplies Needed

As you begin on this new journey to prepare your baby's food, take note of some common cooking utensils and supplies, which will be useful in helping you with this process. To begin with, the usual products needed include a measuring cup, measuring spoons, a cutting board, a paring knife, a potato peeler, a grater, stirring utensils, an egg poacher, a potato masher, and a sharpie pen.

With regard to pots and pans, you'll need a cookie sheet, a sauté pan, and for those instances when you're making an entire meal for the family, a large frying pan and boiling pot. You'll also need a medium sauce pan that has a lid. You'll also want to purchase a vegetable steamer that fits into the pan with the lid on.

Wow! While that sounds like a mouthful, you'll find that you likely have everything you need right in your drawers or cupboards already. Preparing homemade baby food is something you can enjoy every day or once in a while, but one thing for sure; with each recipe you prepare, love is included in the recipe.

At first, as you introduce solid foods to your infant or toddler, you'll most likely be serving very plain veggies and fruits as he gets used to eating new flavors. This includes textured fruits. Vegetables can be prepared by steaming or baking in the oven. For most vegetables, you'll find that steaming works best. However, for vegetables such as potatoes and squash, you may opt to bake in the oven. The healthiest mode of preparation is to steam the vegetables. In order to do this, you'll need a steaming basket that fits into a medium sized saucepan with a lid. For vegetables, such as sweet potatoes, Yukon potatoes, and squash, you can also bake in your oven.

In order to puree your baby's food, you'll need a blender, a food processor, or a mixer, especially if you'd like to get a fine, smooth puree. Some foods can be mashed with a fork or a potato masher. However, if the food is at all stringy, you'll need something more to get rid of the texture. Once you have blended or mixed your food, you might want to use a metal sieve or strainer to exclude things like seeds or rind that may have gotten into the mixture. The sieve will be useful when making smoothies, as sometimes particle of peel can get into the mix. You'll also use your strainer for rinsing pasta and possibly rice or risotto.

The final supplies that you'll need will be used for the storage of your baby's food, once it has been prepared. Most people opt to use plastic ice cube trays, which come with attachable lids. These provide a handy way to portion out servings that also allow for easy access in the future. Each ice cube hole holds about one ounce of food, which forms into the shape of a cube. Ziploc freezer bags can be used to store these individual cubes of food once they have been completely frozen so that you can access the ice cube trays to make more food. Also, when food is stored in the refrigerator, it's best to keep it covered, as this will prevent other refrigerator smells from getting on your food and will help to maintain freshness. Individual food items can be wrapped in wax paper or cellophane wrap, but ensure that the item is completely covered and sealed.

Blenders vs. Food Processors

You have several options available when it comes to blenders or food processors. These range from hand-turned food mills to electric food mills, emulsion blenders, Cuisinart, and all-in-one baby food makers. Recently, many have opted to use the Baby Bullet and have been very happy with this product. On the other hand, a Cuisinart or good blender will work just as well. In addition, you can use either of these items for other cooking projects. It's probably best to stay away from the all-in-one product, as there are too many opportunities for one part to break. However, this product might work well if you're living in a small home with limited counter space. Before investing a large amount of money in any one product, think about how serious you are about making your own baby food and how long you will be doing this so that you don't end up with a product that is never used.

Storing Homemade Food

Refrigeration

When making your own baby food, it's important to follow guidelines with regard to refrigerating and freezing your food. If cooked foods are not refrigerated in a timely manner, harmful bacteria are likely to grow. Foods should be refrigerated or frozen within two hours of preparation or purchase. If the food is being kept in an environment where the temperature is over ninety degrees, then freeze or refrigerate within one hour of preparation or purchase.

The maximum time to leave fresh meat, poultry, and fish in the refrigerator is about two days. If you don't plan to use such products within two days, go ahead and freeze to preserve freshness. Lamb, pork, and veal can be left in the refrigerator for a little longer, up to five days prior to freezing. You may also opt to prepare smaller portions so that you don't need to freeze your baby's food. If you choose this option, you can expect to prepare new food every couple of days. You might want to keep a few portions saved in the freezer as a backup for those days when you cannot get out to the store or take time to make your baby's food due to the special circumstances of that day.

Some people opt to bake a sweet potato and use half one day, then freeze and save the other half for another day. The frozen half can be saved in a freezer bag. Remember to let the potato cool before storing it in the freezer.

It's not a good idea to put hot steaming food in your freezer, as this may impact the overall temperature of your freezer, which in turn may affect the rest of the foods stored in your freezer. When you're preparing your infant's food, you need to store those foods in the freezer within two to three hours of preparation. This allows some time for foods that are hotter to cool prior to placing them in the freezer. If you don't plan on freezing your foods, you can leave them in the refrigerator up to three days, maximum. Food that has been pureed should not be kept in the refrigerator for more than two days, as these types of foods have a higher tendency to develop bacteria. Remember - if in doubt, toss it out. It's always better to err on the side of caution when it comes to feeding your infant.

When serving the food that you have prepared for your infant, always serve some into a separate bowl or plate, using a clean spoon. Don't dip the spoon that your baby is eating into the food in the storage container, as this could possibly contaminate the food. The saliva left on your baby's spoon could create an optimum environment for bacteria to thrive and grow.

Freezing

In order to keep food for a longer period of time, as well as offer greater access to this food when needed, many mothers opt to freeze the food that they make for their babies. Baby food should only be kept in the freezer for one month. Discard after this time has elapsed.

Frozen food is easy to use. Just thaw and reheat, either on the stove or in the microwave oven. The most popular method used for freezing food is to put the food into ice cube trays, as mentioned earlier. Fill it just as if you were filling the tray with water to make ice. Once the tray is full and the food is cool enough to freeze, cover the tray with a lid or with a freezer bag and then store it in the freezer. I don't recommend using aluminum foil, as bits of this can tear off and get into your baby's food.

When your food is frozen solid, you can take it out of the trays and store it in a Ziploc freezer bag. This will help to maintain freshness, as well as prevent the food from picking up odors from other foods in your freezer. Be certain to mark the bags with a sharpie marker, including what the food is and the date that it was made. Some foods look so much alike in terms of texture and color that it may be difficult to distinguish certain foods from each other later!

Nutrient-Rich Foods

As you're planning your meals for your infant, you'll want to make choices that include nutrient-rich foods. In this section, we'll look at various nutrients considered indispensable for a balanced diet. We'll also describe which foods are high in specific vitamins and/or nutrients.

To begin with, some of the most nutrient-rich foods include avocado, beans, lentils, cheese, eggs, salmon, turkey, yogurt, tofu, oatmeal, and whole grain products. These foods also have many healing effects as a result of their natural minerals. You probably hear a lot of talk about avocados, salmon, and oatmeal in relation to heart health. While eggs are given a bad rap for their fat content, they are actually a great source of protein, as well as very easy to prepare.

The other benefit to making your own baby food is that you can enrich the dishes you make by adding some natural ingredients. For example, enrich certain recipes by adding flax seed oil, ground flax, sunflower, or sesame seeds. This works well with smoothies and some purees. Three common seeds that can be ground up and added to your baby's food are:

Flax seed

Flax seed is high in lignans, which is an anti-oxidant known to fight cancer, diabetes, heart disease, and arthritis. Flax seed is very high in Omega-3 fatty acids, which are an essential nutrient for a healthy diet (which most people do not eat enough of). Omega 3 fatty acids are needed for brain, skin, nervous system, and circulatory system development. They are also known to help prevent Multiple Sclerosis, Fibromyalgia, cancer, and weight gain. Flax seed has a total of twenty-seven anti-cancer agents found in its lignans. Just to give you a sense of how rich this nutrient source is, note that flax seed has 100 times more lignans than other notable food sources. However, you will find more lignans in the actual ground seed than you will find in the flax seed oil. A note for mothers - lignans found in flax, known as phyto-estrogens, can help balance female hormones and thus, reduce symptoms of PMS and other female hormonal disorders. Flax is a good source of potassium, calcium, magnesium, zinc, copper, vitamin A, and several B vitamins. You can begin introducing flax into your baby's diet at about eight months of age. *Do not give your baby more than three teaspoons of flax per day.*

Pumpkin Seeds

Pumpkin seeds are a good source of zinc, magnesium, phosphorus, manganese, copper, and iron. Pumpkin seeds also provide high amounts of Omega-3 fatty acids, which as stated earlier, help to prevent several medical problems, including ADHD, high blood pressure, as well as strengthening the body's immune system. Being that pumpkin contains phyto-sterols in large amounts, they can also help to reduce cholesterol levels.

Sesame Seeds

Sesame seeds are high in phyto-nutrients such as Omega-6 fatty acids. They contain anti-oxidants, minerals, vitamins, and fibers that help prevent cancer as well as contribute to overall wellness. Sesame seeds can help to lower bad cholesterol (LDL) and increase good cholesterol (HDL) in your blood, due to their being comprised of the mono-unsaturated fatty-acid, oleic acid. Sesame seeds are a good source of folic acid, riboflavin, and niacin, as well as several B vitamins. Niacin helps reduce LDL levels in your blood and enhances GABA activity in the brain, which helps to reduce anxiety and neurosis. These seeds are high in protein, which aids in physical growth and development. Other minerals found in sesame seeds include calcium, iron, magnesium, and selenium; all of which contribute to the development of red blood cells, hormone production, and regulating the activity of cardiac and skeletal muscle activities. Being that sesame seeds also have a connection to food allergies, it is important that you wait until your infant is at least six months old to introduce these into his diet. In addition, if you have a family history of food allergies or your baby currently has eczema, it's best that you consult your pediatrician prior to feeding these to your baby.

Protein

Protein has many important roles in keeping your body strong and healthy. Protein contributes to the growth and repair of body tissues, aids in transporting other nutrients to cells, and helps with the formation of enzymes, hormones, and neurotransmitters. While people can eat a great deal of protein, if they lack the necessary enzymes to digest this protein, it will not be absorbed into their system. This is where foods such as ground flax seed can help. It's important to note that the flax seed must be in ground form in order for the enzymes to be activated.

Potassium

Potassium helps your cells and muscles to function, and also helps your body maintain a natural balance of fluids. Without potassium in your system, you will die. Some signs that suggest inadequate potassium levels include cramping, anxiety, drowsiness, thirst, and fatigue. Some good sources of potassium include broccoli, cabbage, cauliflower, bananas, watermelon, winter squash, potatoes, grapes, peaches, nectarines, green beans, and apples.

Carotenoids

Carotenoids along with bio-flavonoids give colors to fruits and vegetables. They are natural chemicals with nutritive properties that exist in the pigment of colors for plants and animals. Carotenoids can help reduce the damage caused by free radicals as well as prevent cell tissue and genetic damage. They help to boost your immune system and may help prevent diseases such as cancer. Carotenoids are found in sweet corn, onions, apricots, and blueberries.

Beta Carotene

Beta-carotene is an important carotenoid, which your body transforms into vitamin A. It actually has a built-in mechanism that only allows your body to make as much vitamin A as it needs. Beta-carotene is found in sweet potatoes and mangoes.

Vitamin A

Vitamin A aids in the development of our skin, eyes, immune system, and other parts of our body. It can be used to treat eye diseases such as glaucoma or macular degeneration. It has many healing uses for disorders such as eczema, cold sores, and wounds. It's also thought to prevent heart disease, slow down the aging process, and to reduce heart disease. Vitamin A is found in broccoli, eggplant, asparagus, cantaloupe, avocado, Brussels sprouts, grape fruit, watermelon, apples, green beans, nectarines, cherries, spinach, pears, cucumbers, and grapes. It's also found in eggs, whole milk, butter, and some fish.

Vitamin C

Vitamin C is best known for its ability to help strengthen your immune system. Vitamin C fights off viruses and bacteria. Specifically, it can help to prevent heart disease, stroke, cancer, and eye diseases such as glaucoma. Vitamin C is found in many fruits and vegetables. These include but are not limited to cauliflower, asparagus, bananas, eggplant, grape fruit, broccoli, avocado, watermelon, potatoes, cucumbers pears, green peppers, red peppers, peach, nectarines, green beans, and apples.

Calcium

Calcium helps you to develop strong bones and teeth. It's found in cantaloupe, grapefruit, broccoli, spinach, milk, coconut milk, cheese, spinach, kale, white beans, soy beans, salmon, trout, some cereals, and some orange juices.

Helpful Hints for Cooking

Vegetables

The three primary methods for cooking your baby's vegetables are steaming, baking, and boiling. Using any of these methods, you can cook large portions at a time. This is helpful, especially when you plan to freeze portions of food. For most vegetables, excluding sweet potatoes, squash, and pumpkin, steaming is the preferred method, as it allows the vegetables to maintain the most nutrients. Baking works best for pumpkin, squash, and sweet potato, as it allows you to add other flavorings, as well as creating a nice texture for the vegetable.

If you opt to use boiling as your method of choice for cooking vegetables, you can start by using flavored stocks, such as chicken, vegetable, or beef stock. Any of these will add a nice flavor to your vegetables.

Once the boiling process is completed, set the cooking liquid aside, and you can add it to your purees. However, do not do this with cooked carrots. You can also use the microwave to cook some vegetables, although you will not always get desired texture using this method. If you use the microwave to reheat food, always use a glass container, as plastic is known to release toxins when microwaved.

Once your vegetables are cooked, remove them from the pan and put them in the blender or food processor that you'll use for pureeing. If you have a large portion of food to puree, only fill the container half way for better results. Add some liquid to the puree mixture. This can be breast milk, formula, or the cooking liquid from boiling your vegetables. This will help you to get a smoother, creamier texture for the food, which is easier for younger kids to eat. This liquid also contains nutrients from the vegetables, released during the cooking process. If you plan to freeze the batch of vegetables, you might opt to hold off on adding the liquid and instead add it when you're ready to feed your infant. This is up to you.

Seasoning

As you read through reports and articles on cooking baby food, you'll hear much of the same advice repeated, especially surrounding the use of salt, pepper, and other seasonings, as well as butter and other ingredients.

First off, most recipes state to use unsalted butter, as many experts feel that babies don't need the extra salt found in butter. Exposing them to saltier foods at a young age will create a lifelong need for salty food. Therefore, as you read the recipes in this book, you'll note that we have not recommended you use unsalted butter; however this is an implied suggestion for you to keep in mind with any of the recipes which call for butter.

The same goes for salt and pepper. Generally, the recipes in this book suggest that you use salt and pepper to taste. You can either forgo the use of salt and pepper all together or add a dash as per your taste. The younger your baby is, the more important it is to avoid salt, pepper, and other spices however, as his system is just developing and getting used to solid foods. Around age seven months, it is safe to include cinnamon, pepper, and garlic powder. You can actually add a cinnamon stick to boiling water as you cook your fruits and vegetables, and then remove the stick prior to pureeing.

After age one, your baby will be better prepared to consume a range of spices. However, it is still recommended that you go easy on the flavoring in his food. Also, if your baby has already been diagnosed with acid reflux, this gives you even more of a reason to be careful with spices, as they might further exacerbate this condition.

The nice thing about this stage of life is that you and your baby are more familiar with one another and by the age of one, you know what your baby's expressions mean. They are better able to communicate, scream for your attention, make truly sour faces, and wave their arms in delight! The silly times with the airplane or train spoons are a memory that has lasted a lifetime for me and is one of the most special times in my life.

Onions and Garlic

Many of the recipes in this book call for use of chopped onion and garlic. While onion and garlic truly adds flavor to the food, they may not go over so well with your baby's taste buds. One way to get around this is to forgo the chopping or mincing of the onion and rather cook your food with a whole clove of garlic or large chunk of onion, which can then be easily removed when it comes time to serving your meal. This works especially well with rice and soups.

Meats

In this book, you'll find that not many recipes contain beef. That's because with beef, it's easiest to take a portion of the meat that you have cooked for yourself and puree it or chop it into small pieces and serve to your baby. A couple of beef options which work well for families is to cook a chuck roast, which can later be shredded for barbecue beef, tacos, or burritos. This is easy enough to do. Just fill a large boiling pot with water, garlic, salt, and pepper, place the meat in it and slow-boil for two hours. Set the broth aside to use for cooking future dishes.

Another great time-saving idea is to make a roast. You can serve your baby and yourself that night and then use the same meat for future meals, such as sandwiches, hash, tacos, or casseroles. Keep in mind, if you're cooking a fancy dish such as beef stroganoff for your family, but you feel that the dish is too much for baby, set aside some of ingredients, such as the noodles, beef, and sour cream, and puree these together.

Chicken and turkey are two very popular baby foods. They both go well with a number of side dishes, including sweet potatoes, rice, and pasta. Chicken breasts are very quick and easy to cook. You can boil one on the stove for about twenty minutes and even add some carrots or peas to the water as it's cooking for added flavor and nutritional content.

Using Formula or Breast Milk

To add extra nutrients to your baby's food, you can also include formula or breast milk, which also help to liquefy the food a little more, allowing for easier eating, especially as your baby is first transitioning to solid foods. The flavor of the formula or breast milk is also familiar to your baby so they are likely to help him enjoy the taste of this new food a little more.

Usually, when parents start to give their infant cereal, formula, or breast milk is added in order to make the cereal less thick. Some parents opt to thin their baby's purees prior to freezing. Just remember that if you do this, you should not refreeze frozen food that has been already thawed.

Another option for thinning foods like vegetables is to use the water that they were originally cooked in. Steamed or boiled vegetables make their own broth or stock. This is recommended for most vegetables, except for carrots.

Squash

Squash is a great starter food for your infant. You can introduce squash at six to eight months of age. The nice, mild taste with a hint of sweetness and gold to orange coloring make it very appealing to baby. You have many different types of squash to choose from. Since squash has a hard shell, it's one of those foods that is immune to pesticide absorption.

Winter squash is named for when it is available, as well as how it matures and ripens on the vine. Of the winter squash family, butternut and acorn are two of the most popular choices for your baby. Winter squash is primarily available during the months of November through December. You can start giving your baby winter squash at eight months of age.

A few additional and popular types of squash are listed as follows. Acorn squash is shaped like an acorn and is usually dark green or yellow or orange. Acorn squash is naturally sweet and tastes good when baked with brown sugar and a touch of cinnamon. Butternut squash is more bell or pear shaped and is light colored like, well, butter! The flavor of this squash is also sweet with a slight nutty taste.

Squash is high in vitamin A and calcium. Squash can be pureed into a very fine mixture. Use a sharp knife to cut the squash in half lengthwise. Scoop out the seeds and discard. Lay the squash face down in a baking dish with about one inch of water covering the bottom of the pan. Cook for about 40 minutes at 400 degrees. It's preferable to bake or roast squash in the oven, as this process retains the most nutrients. This also prevents you from having to peel and cube the squash, required when it is boiled.

Squash goes well with the following foods: apples, peaches, pears, carrots, parsnip, rice, lentils, chicken, beef, and pork. Cinnamon, brown sugar, ginger, and nutmeg can all be used to add a little flavor to your squash dishes.

Butternut or Acorn Squash Puree

Ingredients:

1 acorn or butternut squash

Water or breast milk to moisten

As described above, cut the squash in half lengthwise and scoop out the seeds. Put one to two inches of water in a medium baking pan and place the squash face down in the pan. Bake in a 400 degree oven for about 45 minutes. The skin or shell of the squash should be puckered at this point. Scoop the meat out of the squash and place it in your blender or food processor. Add a small amount of water or breast milk to moisten the mixture. Blend using the puree setting for about thirty seconds or until you notice the desired texture has been achieved.

Baked Apple and Acorn Squash

If you like happy faces, you'll love this recipe! When I served this recipe to each of my children, arms would start to wave and the babbles and smiles started. To be honest, it's one of my favorite recipes as well, as I was my children's connoisseur of everything that went into their mouths!

Ingredients:

1 acorn squash

2 or 3 McIntosh apples

Dash of cinnamon

Prepare the apples by coring, peeling, and dicing. Cut the acorn squash in half and scoop out the seeds. Place about one inch of water in a medium baking pan and place the two halves of the squash face up in the pan. Add the diced apples into the center holes of squash and sprinkle with a dash of cinnamon. Pour a small amount of water over the apples to keep them moist as they bake. Cover the pan with a lid or tin foil. Bake in a 400-degree oven for about 45 minutes. Scoop the squash meat out of the shell and place in your blender or food processor. Puree until desired texture is achieved. Serve with rice.

Baked Squash Bowls

The combination of ingredients in this recipe really makes a tasty dish. While each of us is aware of the great appeal of applesauce and raisins, not all of us are aware of the great taste when acorn or butternut squash is included. This is another great recipe and one that I used as a dessert!

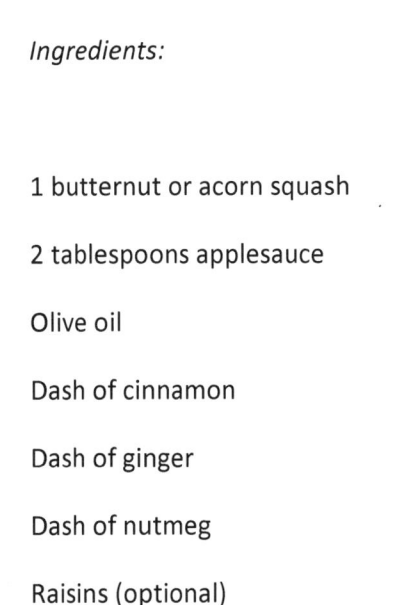

Ingredients:

1 butternut or acorn squash

2 tablespoons applesauce

Olive oil

Dash of cinnamon

Dash of ginger

Dash of nutmeg

Raisins (optional)

Cut the butternut or acorn squash in half lengthwise and scoop out the seeds. Put about one to two inches of water in the bottom of a medium baking dish. Braise the inside of the squash with olive oil and place face up, shell down in the same baking dish. Pour the applesauce into the inside of the squash. Add raisins if you choose. Bake in a 400-degree oven for about 45 minutes. The skin will pucker when it is cooked. You can serve as is or scoop out the squash, puree, and serve with the applesauce. Kids find it fun to eat straight out of the shell.

Butternut Squash and Potato Puree

If you have yet to introduce whole milk, then please use the four-day rule, and don't introduce any other new foods until you are sure your baby does not have a reaction. While the chives are optional in this recipe, they are a great addition and one that I think you'll find your child will like.

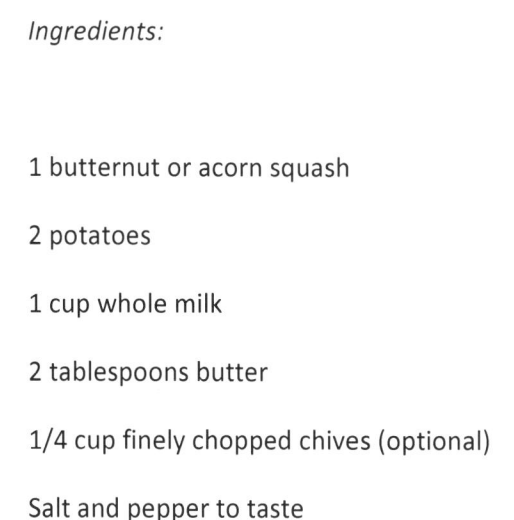

Ingredients:

1 butternut or acorn squash

2 potatoes

1 cup whole milk

2 tablespoons butter

1/4 cup finely chopped chives (optional)

Salt and pepper to taste

Cut the squash in half lengthwise and scoop out the seeds. Peel the shell off the squash and cut into small cubes. Peel the potatoes, wash very well, and cut into three parts. Fill a large pot about two thirds full with water and add ½ teaspoon salt. Put the potatoes and squash in the pot, bring the water to a boil, and cook for about 30 to 45 minutes. Drain all of the water, except for about one cup and add the yogurt and butter. Use a potato peeler to mash the potatoes and squash to your desired texture. Add chives, salt, and pepper if you choose.

Stuffed Squash

This is a great fruits and veggies recipe, another that you can expect to see the arms waving in excitement! This is one that was always gobbled right down with my youngest.

Ingredients:

2 acorn squash

1 tsp. canola oil

1 medium apple, peeled, cored, and diced

1/2 small onion, finely chopped

1/2 celery stalk, diced

1/2 tsp. dried thyme

1/2 tsp. dried sage

2 cups cooked whole-grain rice

1/2 cup dried apricots, chopped

1/4 cup dried cranberries

1/4 cup apple cider (or juice)

Cut both of the squash lengthwise in half and scoop out seeds. Put one to two inches of water in a medium or large baking dish. Place the squash halves face down in the dish. Bake at 400 degrees for about 45 minutes. Set aside and cool on a large cookie sheet.

Now work on the stuffing. Finely dice the apple, onions, and celery, place in a medium skillet with the Canola oil and sauté for about two to three minutes. Add the thyme and sage to the mixture, and then stir in the cooked rice, apricots, and dried cranberries. Add the apple cider and cook until it is almost evaporated.

Place cooled squash on a large nonstick cookie sheet. Fill the center of the squash with the stuffing mix. Bake in the oven at 400 degrees for an additional 20 minutes. Scoop out the stuffing and the squash and mix in your blender or food processor until pureed. You can also mash the squash and mix with the stuffing. Return the mixture to the empty squash shell and serve in the shell.

Cinnamon Squash Puree

Ingredients:

4-5 ounces chopped butternut or acorn squash

Water

1/2 cinnamon stick

In a medium sauce pan, fill two-thirds full of water. Bring the water to a boil and add the squash and the cinnamon stick. Cook until the squash is soft, and then discard the cinnamon stick. Put the squash in your blender or food processor and puree for about 30 seconds. Add some of the cooking liquid or breast milk if the mixture needs moistening.

Carrot, Butternut, and Leek Puree

Ingredients:

1 carrot

1/2 leek, thinly sliced

1 1/2 cup butternut squash

1 teaspoon butter

Water for steaming

Cut the squash in half lengthwise. Scoop out the seeds and place the squash face down in a medium baking dish with about one to two inches of water. Place the squash in the oven at 400 degrees and cook for 45 minutes. While the squash is cooking - peel, clean, and chop the carrot and place in your steam basket. Thinly slice the leek and place about fifteen slices in the steam basket. Steam the carrots and leeks for about five to 10 minutes or until the carrots are softened.

Scoop out the cooked squash and place in your blender or food processor. Add the steamed carrots, leaks, and butter to the mixture. Puree until a smooth consistency is reached. Add water or breast milk if the mixture is too dry.

Butternut Squash and Cauliflower Puree

Ingredients:

Half a butternut squash

5 cauliflower florets

1 teaspoon butter

Preheat oven to 350 degrees. Spray a baking dish with non-stick cooking spray or grease with butter. Cut the butternut squash in half and place face down in the baking dish. Cook the squash for 40 minutes or until softened. Clean the cauliflower and steam in your steamer basket for 9 minutes. Remove and set aside. Remove the squash and scoop into a bowl. Add the squash, the cauliflower, and the butter to your food processor or blender and puree to desired texture. Add some breast milk or a splash of water if needed.

Smoothies

Smoothies are a wonderful way to get your baby to try a number of different fruits in a very yummy concoction. You'll most likely indulge in these treats as you make them. Just think about how popular products such as Jamba Juice have become. You'll be amazed to see how easily these are made, as well as how many variations of recipes can be created. The other good thing about smoothies is that they offer very good opportunities for you to add nutrients such as flax seed oil, protein powder, or multi mineral protein to baby's diet.

Cinnamon and nutmeg can be added after eight months of age. After age one, the following products can be added: berries, mango, papaya, pomegranate seeds, spinach leaves, tofu, wheat germ, and whey wheat powder pick.

Smoothies have been a big treat in my family for years. From the time my oldest first began to drink them until now (she is now five years old!); the drinks are something that she gets excited about. There are so many wonderful combinations of fruits and veggies to use so definitely don't be afraid to experiment.

When I built my children's nutritional foundation, I wasn't quite aware of the influence it would have on them as an individual at such a young age. Smoothies in our home are accessible at all times of the day and on all occasions - for backyard playtime, school snacks, when grandma comes to visit, and even with breakfast. They're a fantastic way to get fruits and vegetables into a child in a way that's fun *and* tasty.

Banana Ginger Smoothie

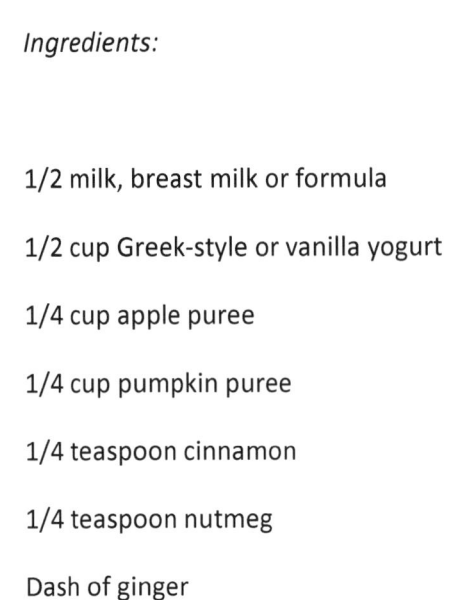

Ingredients:

1/2 milk, breast milk or formula

1/2 cup Greek-style or vanilla yogurt

1/4 cup apple puree

1/4 cup pumpkin puree

1/4 teaspoon cinnamon

1/4 teaspoon nutmeg

Dash of ginger

1 sliced banana

Add all of the ingredients to your blender and mix together until smooth. Serve immediately. You can also add breast milk or formula to this recipe if desired.

Pumpkin, Apple, and Banana Surprise

This is the perfect smoothie recipe to enjoy any time of the day. With my children and children of family and friends, this is one recipe that I can always make and never have a problem with anyone enjoying it!

Ingredients:

1 sliced banana

1/2 cup plain yogurt

1/4 cup pureed pumpkin

1/4 cup apple puree

1/4 teaspoon nutmeg

1/4 teaspoon cinnamon

Dash of ginger

Add all of the ingredients to your blender and mix together until smooth. Serve immediately. You can also add breast milk or formula to this recipe if desired.

Pumpkin and Banana Smoothie

This recipe is also great to freeze! If your baby is able to hold a Popsicle, this will be a summer Popsicle hit.

Ingredients:

1 cup plain yogurt

2 tablespoons pureed pumpkin

1 banana sliced

Dash of cinnamon

Add all of the ingredients to your blender and mix together until smooth. Serve immediately. You can also add breast milk or formula to this recipe if desired.

Pina-Coco-Ba Smoothie

I found coconut to be a taste that my children either liked or disliked - my little one that disliked it seemed to be able to taste it no matter what it was in! If your little one has a dislike for coconut, you can substitute with whole milk.

Ingredients:

1 sliced banana

1/4 cup coconut milk

1/4 cup pineapple juice

1/2 cup apple juice

Add all of the ingredients to your blender and mix together until smooth. Serve immediately. You can also add breast milk or formula to this recipe if desired.

Bananarama

Ingredients:

1/2 sliced banana

1/2 cup coconut milk

1/2 cup frozen vanilla or Greek yogurt

1/2 cup ice

Add all of the ingredients to your blender, adding the ice last. Mix together until smooth. Serve immediately. You can also add breast milk or formula to this recipe if desired.

Raz-a-Taz

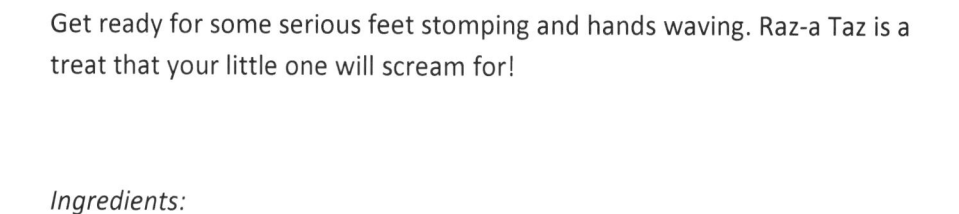

Get ready for some serious feet stomping and hands waving. Raz-a Taz is a treat that your little one will scream for!

Ingredients:

1/2 cup raspberries

1/4 cup blueberries

1/2 cup Greek yogurt

1/2 cup orange juice

Add all of the ingredients to your blender and mix together until smooth. Serve immediately. You can also add breast milk or formula to this recipe if desired.

Peach Foamy

This is great on hot summer afternoons! My oldest considers this smoothie to be her "special" treat!

Ingredients:

1 cup peeled and sliced fresh peaches

1/2 cup coconut milk or whole milk

1/2 cup Greek yogurt

1/2 cup strawberries

1/4 teaspoon cinnamon

Add all of the ingredients to your blender and mix together until smooth. Serve immediately. You can also add breast milk or formula to this recipe if desired. You may run this through a sieve to remove the strawberry seeds.

Pineapple Delight

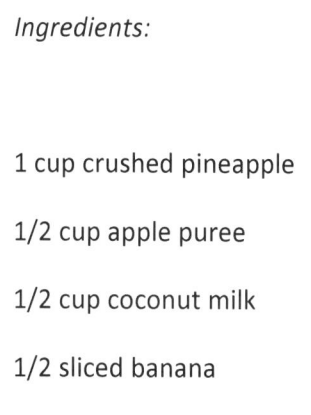

Ingredients:

1 cup crushed pineapple

1/2 cup apple puree

1/2 cup coconut milk

1/2 sliced banana

1/2 cup orange juice

Add all of the ingredients to your blender and mix together until smooth. Serve immediately. You can also add breast milk or formula to this recipe if desired.

Watermelon Smoothie

There is something about kids and watermelon! You'll find that this is a smoothie not likely to be turned down by anyone.

Ingredients:

1½ cup seeded watermelon

1/2 cup strawberries

1/2 of a peach, sliced and peeled

1/2 cup vanilla or Greek yogurt

Add all of the ingredients to your blender and mix together until smooth. Serve immediately. You can also add breast milk or formula to this recipe if desired. You may run this through a sieve to remove the strawberry seeds.

Banana Raspberry Smoothie

Ingredients:

1 sliced banana

1 cup frozen raspberries

1/2 cup Greek yogurt

1/2 cup orange juice

Add all of the ingredients to your blender and mix together until smooth. Serve immediately. You can also add breast milk or formula to this recipe if desired.

Mango Smoothie

Ingredients:

1 mango, sliced, peeled, and pitted

1/2 cup lime juice

1/2 cup orange juice

1/2 cup crushed ice

Add all of the ingredients to your blender and mix together until smooth. Serve immediately. You can also add breast milk or formula to this recipe if desired.

Dips

Dips are fun for parents and kids! In our home, we dip everything from grapes to pretzels to veggies and everything else between! I am a true supporter of "fun" foods and dips are the answer in this home no matter what the occasion.

Dips are great way to introduce your toddler to new and healthy food ingredients. Your child will probably be ready to eat dips around eighteen months of age, dependent on his teeth and ability to chew. This truly is an autonomous activity for your infant, which will help them to feel more independent. Children love being able to dip their own food and this becomes a fun game for them. Thus, you might want to give them their own bowl for dipping.

As a parent, you can take advantage of this fact and prepare dips that are high in protein, as well as other nutrients such as calcium and vitamins A and D. Popular ingredients for dips include avocado, pureed fruit, sour cream, Cream cheese, cheese, yogurt, buttermilk dressing, refried beans, chick-peas, and Tahini.

As you prepare any of these dips, low-fat products may be substituted for whole products, such as milk, cheese, and sour cream. Yogurt may be substituted for sour cream or vice versa. If your baby is comfortable with eating mild spices, then prepare the recipe with these included. If not, prepare the recipe excluding the spices. Set a small amount aside for your infant and then spice the rest of the batch to taste for yourself and the rest of your family.

Your choice of foods to serve with each dip will depend on your child's ability to chew and swallow food. For picky eaters, dips are a great addition to the diet. Kids tend to find dips "silly" food. I love watching my group at the table with fruits, veggies, and dips with the giggles and laughs as they find enjoyment in taking an ordinary food and dressing it up to be truly tasteful! They're a wonderful way to help children enjoy fruits and vegetables.

Guacamole (After one year)

This recipe makes one whole batch. However, prior to spicing, set some aside for your baby. Use a little lemon juice to keep the avocado from turning brown.

Ingredients:

2 whole ripe avocados, cut in half, peeled, and pitted

1 whole lemon

1/4 cup grated Monterey Jack cheese (optional)

1 tablespoon finely chopped Spanish onion

Tabasco sauce to taste (You may use chili juice)

Salt and pepper to taste

Mash the avocado until it has an almost creamy texture, removing large chunks. Squeeze the lemon over the avocado and add the grated cheese. Set aside about ¼ cup of this mixture for your baby. Add the onions, salt, pepper, and tobacco or chili juice. Mix together and serve immediately or cover and store in the refrigerator until ready to use. This dip is actually best if prepared when you're ready to use it.

Cucumber Yogurt Dip

Although I have cucumbers listed, the kids and I enjoy this dip with just about everything! The lemon and garlic give the yogurt a truly nice flavor that complements most veggies. If your little ones are anything like mine, then cucumbers are the hit of the party!

Ingredients:

8 ounces Greek yogurt

1/2 cucumber

1 glove of garlic

1/2 tablespoon olive oil

1/2 tablespoon lemon juice

Dice cucumber into small pieces, remove seeds. Combine yogurt, cucumbers, oil, and lemon juice. Mix well, chill, and serve cold with banana bread (Indian bread) or thinly slices sourdough bread.

Bean Dip

I have yet to meet a child that doesn't like bean dip! This dip is so delicious, I serve it at parties! You can also make homemade tortillas by adding a bit of oil to a pan and then frying a few tortilla strips. The kids will think you're a master chef!

Ingredients:

1 can non-fat organic refried beans

1/2 cup sour cream

1/2 cup grated Cheddar cheese

1/2 cup chopped green onions (optional)

Warm the refried beans on the stove until hot throughout. Pour into a serving dish and stir in sour cream, Cheddar cheese, and green onions. Serve with flour or corn tortillas or tortilla chips.

Hummus

This recipe makes one whole batch. However, prior to spicing, set some aside for your baby.

Ingredients:

4 garlic cloves

2 cups of chick peas, cleaned, and drained

1/3 cup Tahini

2 lemons

2 tablespoons water

1½ teaspoons kosher salt

Tabasco or hot sauce to taste

Using your blender or food processor, add the garlic to the holding container, and grind until finely minced. Add in the garlic, chick peas, Tahini, lemon juice, and water. Puree until it is a course mixture. Set about ¼ cup aside for your baby, then add the remaining ingredients, salt and Tabasco to serve for the rest of your family. Serve with cut up pita bread or pita chips.

Strawberry and Peach Fruit Dip

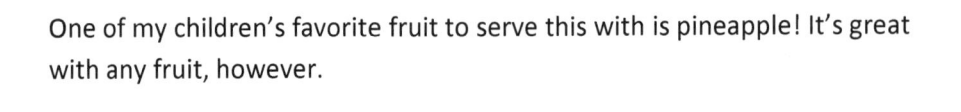

One of my children's favorite fruit to serve this with is pineapple! It's great with any fruit, however.

Ingredients:

2 cups fresh peaches, sliced, peeled, and pitted

1½ cups of fresh strawberries, tops taken off

1 tablespoon lemon juice

Using your blender or food processor, add the peaches, strawberries, and lemon juice. Puree until the desired consistency. Serve with cut fruit.

Creamy Lemon Dip

Ingredients:

2 cups sour cream

1 package instant vanilla pudding

1/4 cup milk

4 teaspoons lemon juice

In a mixing bowl, combine the sour cream, pudding mix milk, and lemon juice. Mix all ingredients and serve chilled with assorted fruits for dipping.

Cream Cheese Dip

I can serve bell pepper plain and there's no excitement. When paired with this dip, the entire house floods the table! This is a great tasting dip that can spice up any veggie!

Ingredients:

16 ounces Cream cheese

1 cup whole milk or Greek yogurt

2 tablespoons lemon juice

Garlic powder and onion powder to taste

With a hand mixer, blend the Cream cheese, milk or yogurt, and lemon juice together until the consistency is smooth. Set aside some for your infant. With remaining, add spices to taste. Serve with yellow and red peppers or jicama sticks.

Cottage Cheese Dip

Ingredients:

2 cups Cottage cheese

1 cup grated Cheddar cheese

1/2 cup Greek yogurt or sour cream

Dab of horseradish

Dash of Worcestershire sauce

Pepper to taste

Place Cottage cheese, grated cheese, and yogurt, mix well. Add the horseradish, Worcestershire sauce, and pepper to taste. Serve with crackers, pita, or cut vegetables.

Avocado

As women and moms, most of us are aware that avocado is a wonder food. Avocados are so popular with my children that I actually have four avocado plants! For the little ones, they are ideal, packed with good fats, anti-oxidants, and other nutrients. Avocados are a fruit option that can be consumed on a daily basis.

Remember, babies need fat so do not avoid this power food due to its fat content. Avocado is good for your baby's brain and physical development and can be introduced at six months of age. Fats, proteins, and carbohydrates are needed for your infant's growth in their first year of life. Avocado is a great food for your baby to eat, as it has a soft texture, which is easy to chew and once mashed and mixed, is very creamy. You can mash up avocado and mix it with applesauce, pears, and yogurt. Other foods that go well with avocado are bananas, zucchini, and chicken.

Avocados have a thick peel so they are one of those fruits that are not susceptible to pesticides. There are two primary types of avocados. It is preferable to use the ones with the darker, thicker green skin rather than those with the thinner skin, as the former have more flavor. You might want to buy your avocados a few days before you're ready to use, as they are not always fully ripened in the store. Try to pick an avocado that is firm, yet with a hint of softness. Avocados that are very mushy may be overripe and may have an odd flavor.

Avocados do not need to be cooked. You can cut them straight from the peel into slices. Some people who opt to freeze avocados put a little lemon juice on them prior to freezing to avoid the fruit turning brown.

Avocado Rolls (Recommended for 2 years old and above)

Ingredients:

1/2 cup short grain rice

2 tablespoons rice vinegar

2 teaspoons salt

2¼ teaspoon sugar

Bamboo sushi mat

Plastic wrap

Nori (Sushi Seaweed Wrap)

Avocado

*Nori can be purchased at Japanese or other kinds of Asian supermarkets. Sometimes found at the Asian section of an American supermarket - ask the clerk.

Rinse the rice thoroughly until it's clear. Boil the rice in water until tender. Remove the rice from the stove and set aside. In a saucepan, combine the rice vinegar, salt, and sugar, cook until hot, but do not allow it to boil. Mix the vinegar with the rice and set aside to cool. This rice is now ready to use as the outside layer of your avocado roll. Cut your avocado into very thin slices, julienne style. Set this aside to be used as the stuffing. You can also use this same rice mixture to make other sushi rolls that contain raw fish such as tuna or salmon.

The next steps involve making your rolls. Start by laying out a piece of plastic wrap on top of your bamboo mat. Next, place a sheet of Nori on top of the plastic. Spread a thin layer of the rice mixture on top of the Nori.

Make certain to leave a thin strip of the Nori uncovered so that you can use it to seal the roll.

Place the slices of avocado on top of the rice mixture. Tightly roll up the Nori and use a dab of rice vinegar to make the two sides of the Nori stick together, making certain that the roll is packed snuggly. You now have one large roll which can be sliced into thin servings. Determine serving slice size based on your baby's size and ability to chew.

Avocado and Cream Cheese Spread

This is truly a spread made for champions! My little ones love this recipe with a passion and will eat it plain or on flour tortillas, toast or pita bread.

Ingredients:

1/2 avocados

1/2 cup Cream cheese

2 tablespoons crushed cheerios or wheat germ

Mash the avocado and Cream cheese together until the mixture is smooth. Add the crushed cheerios or wheat germ. Spread this on pita, toast, or flour tortillas.

Avocado Fruit Salad

Ingredients:

1 ripe avocado

1 banana

1 pear peeled, deseeded, and lightly steamed

2 tablespoons Greek yogurt

Peel and seed both your avocado, banana, and steamed pear. Place in a blender or food processor and puree until the desired texture is reached. Serve with yogurt. For older toddlers, do not puree this mixture and serve the fruits with the yogurt on the side. You can also serve with Mozzarella string cheese.

Avocado Mango Spread

When you see the smiles that cheer "yes," you know that this recipe is a keeper! This is one that my kids ask for at least once a week. It's great on toast or served with fruit.

Ingredients:

1 ripe avocado

1 cup mango

1/4 cup Greek yogurt

1/4 cup apple or pear juice

Peel, seed, and cut the avocado and mango into small cubes and place in a mixing bowl. Mash together with a fork until smooth. Add the yogurt or juice and blend with a whisk until the mixture becomes creamy. Spread this on pita, toast, or flour tortillas. For older kids, you can opt to skip the puree step and serve the fruit in small bite-size chunks that they can chew.

Avocados and Peaches

Simple, but delicious! This recipe will be a favorite summer special!

Ingredients:

3 peaches

1 avocado

Peel, pit, and cut peaches into small cubes. Briefly steam until tender. Peel and seed the avocado, cut into the same size cubes. Blend foods on puree setting until smooth and serve cold.

Avocados and Pears

Ingredients:

2 ripe pears

1 ripe avocado

Peel, seed, and cut up the pear and the avocado into small bits.

Avocado, Cucumber, Tomato, and Cheese Salad (Over 1 year old)

You experience a special feeling when you're able to prepare more advanced food for your children. Like all recipes in this book, you'll find that the ingredients do help to build a healthy foundation of foods they will later enjoy.

Ingredients:

1/4 avocado

1/2 stick of Mozzarella string cheese

1 small plum tomato

1/4 cut cucumber

Cut the avocado into small bite size pieces and place in a medium bowl. String the cheese and cut into bite size pieces and add to the bowl. You can leave the pieces a little bigger for older kids. Dice the tomato into small pieces and add to your bowl. Peel and clean your cucumber and cut into small pieces, add to the bowl. Mix everything together. You can add a dash of balsamic vinegar and salad oil if you choose; however, the salad is very tasty on its own. Prepare the same salad for the rest of your family and add a balsamic dressing.

Bananas

Bananas are sweet and delicious, as they contain an array of vitamins and minerals, including protein, potassium, and vitamins A and C. Bananas are naturally sweet so no added sugar is needed. You can eat them alone, mixed with other fruits, mixed with cereal, or oatmeal. Bananas help lower cholesterol and blood pressure. They can help with sleeplessness and decrease leg cramps. Some people feed their kids bananas at night in order to fill them with calories, as well as help with sleep. You can mash your bananas up or puree. You don't have to remove the seeds as they're so small that they are not a hazard for choking.

Bananas are one food that I can always count on and I think most parents feel the same way. Children love the fruit. I find that in my house, even when I can't get the kids to eat anything else, if they eat a banana, it puts me right at ease.

Bananas Foster

Ingredients:

1 banana

Splash of orange juice

Dash of cinnamon

Two drops of vanilla extract

Slice the banana and set aside. Heat your sauté pan and add all of the ingredients. Sauté the bananas for one minute. Use the back of a fork to mash the ingredients and serve. This is a yummy, simple desert that takes only minutes to make.

Bananas and Pumpkin

This is one of the best recipes to spruce up rice cereal - and you'll likely find that your children eat it for years!

Ingredients:

1/2 cup pumpkin puree

2 bananas

In a medium bowl, mash the bananas, add the pumpkin puree, and mix together. This may also be pureed. Serve with rice cereal.

Banana and Avocado Mix

Ingredients:

1 ripe avocado

1 banana

Peel the avocado and remove the seed. Place halves in a mixing bowl and mash with a potato masher or a fork. Add the peeled banana to the bowl and mash some more. For a smoother texture, you can add a little water and puree. Serve cold.

Hot Bananas

When you want to be a "Superhero Mom," this is definitely the treat to make! This is such a fantastic recipe, the kids will scream for more!

Ingredients:

1 banana

Pure maple syrup to taste

Butter

Pre-heat your oven to 350 degrees. Grease a small baking dish with butter. Peel and cut the banana lengthwise and place each half face up in the baking dish. Rub the bananas with a little butter. Drizzle with the maple syrup. Bake in the oven for 12 minutes. Let stand to cool.

Pumpkin

You can introduce pumpkin into your baby's diet between six and eight months of age. Pumpkins are loaded with many vitamins and nutrients, including vitamin A and beta carotene, both of which help to prevent heart disease and cancer. Pumpkins also contain potassium, protein, iron, and are a good source of fiber. Since pumpkins have a very thick shell, they're not prone to pesticide absorption.

You'll find many different types of pumpkin on the market, but you might want to use pie pumpkins for making your baby's food. This type of pumpkin is smaller and tends to have fewer strings. To avoid getting these strings, don't scrape too close to the shell.

Different ways to cook pumpkin include poaching, boiling, steaming, or baking. The preferred choice is to bake in the oven. When baking, follow steps similar to cooking squash. Do not over bake, as nutrients can be lost in the baking process. It is necessary to cook pumpkins right after they have been opened, as they will develop mold very quickly once they are exposed to the air. After cooking pumpkin, be sure to refrigerate or freeze immediately. You can puree it prior to freezing or you can freeze large chunks of it to cook at a later time. Pumpkins can be served as a pureed dish with a dash of cinnamon or they can be mixed with foods such as chicken, potatoes, or yogurt.

As a mommy, pumpkin has always been one of my most successful foods - and as moms, you know just how many things that pumpkin can be used in. It's a fun food and a healthy food and if your kids are anything like mine, it will be a favorite food! One great event I enjoy with my two older children is that each year, we plant a Halloween pumpkin for each member of the family and the children nurture it until it blooms. This is a great way to start the children on their own healthy eating habits. As an added bonus, you can clean the pumpkin, cook the seeds, and make pumpkin pie together.

Pumpkin Puree

Ingredients:

1 sugar pumpkin

Water

Cinnamon, nutmeg

Cut the pumpkin in half and remove all of the strings. Place face down in a medium baking pan with about an inch or two of water. Bake at 400 degrees for about 45 minutes. When it is cooked, the skin will look puckered or wrinkled. Scrape out the pumpkin meat and place in your blender or food processor. Add a bit of water or breast milk and puree until smooth.

Pumpkin and Apple Puree

Ingredients:

1 sugar pumpkin

3 apples, peeled and cored

Water

Cinnamon, nutmeg

Cut the pumpkin in half and take out the seeds. Cut the pieces of pumpkin into cubes. Peel, core, and slice your apples. Use a medium sauce pan and add three inches of water. Put your steamer in the pot and add the pumpkin cubes and apple slices to the steam basket. Bring the water to a boil and steam the fruit until fully softened. Check regularly to ensure there is enough water in the pot. Once the steaming is complete, put the fruit in your blender or food processor, and puree.

Peach and Pumpkin Puree

My youngest would scream with pleasure when I'd feed her this! There's something about the combination of the pumpkin and the peach that makes a truly special taste and creates a truly happy child!

Ingredients:

1½ cups pumpkin puree

1 pear, peeled, cored, and diced

1peach, peeled, pitted, and diced

Peel, core, and dice the pear. Peal the peach, remove the seed, and dice the fruit into small pieces. Combine the pumpkin puree, peaches, and pears in your blender or food process, then puree. You can also mash with a fork if you prefer.

Pumpkin Puree with Pizzazz

While this is a bit more work than just tossing an ingredient or two into the blender, it's still pretty easy and one that the kids will love!

Ingredients:

2 cups pumpkin meat cut into small cubes

2 tablespoons olive oil

1/4 cup diced onion

2 cups vegetable stock

Pepper

Basil

Nutmeg

Use your medium saucepot and begin by heating the olive oil. Add the onions and pumpkin cubes and sauté until clear and soft. Add the vegetable stock and simmer until the pumpkin is soft and ready to eat. Bring the mixture to a slow simmer and simmer until the squash is tender enough to puree. Add the basil and pepper to taste. Add a dash of nutmeg. Serve with rice or couscous.

Baked Pumpkin Slices

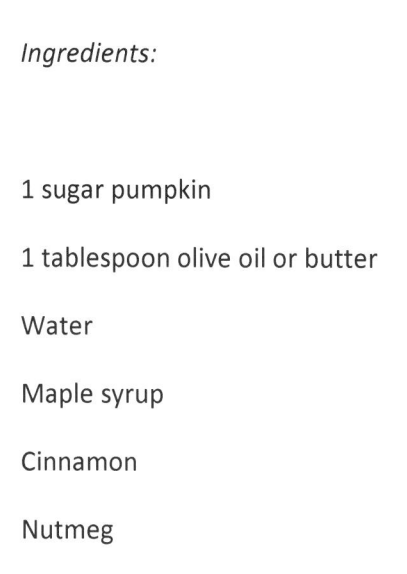

Ingredients:

1 sugar pumpkin

1 tablespoon olive oil or butter

Water

Maple syrup

Cinnamon

Nutmeg

Cut the pumpkin in half and then further cut each half into slices. Baste each slice with a little butter or olive oil and then place each slice on a baking sheet. Drizzle a little water over all of the slices. You can sprinkle with a little brown sugar, cinnamon, or nutmeg. Bake at 400 degrees for 45 minutes.

Pumpkin, Peach, and Avocado

Ingredients:

1/2 cup pumpkin puree

1 avocado, peeled, seeded, and diced

1 ripe peach - peeled, pitted, and diced

Peel, seed, and dice the avocado. Peel, pit, and dice the peach. Combine these fruits and make your pumpkin puree by mashing with the back of a fork.

Pumpkin and Yogurt Puree

Ingredients:

1/2 cup cooked pumpkin cubes

1¼ cup of Greek yogurt

Dash of nutmeg and cinnamon

Place the pumpkin cubes in a food processor or blender and puree until smooth. Pour into a mixing bowl, add the yogurt, and mix well. Add cinnamon and nutmeg to taste.

Sweet Potatoes

Many people are confused over the difference between a sweet potato and a yam. For the most part, they're actually the same. However, yams in the store have the darker reddish peel and the sweet potato has the lighter brownish peel with bright orange meat. Sweet potatoes, as their name suggests, tend to be a little more moist and sweeter than yams. Both yams and sweet potatoes are packed with vitamins and minerals. Sweet potatoes are high in vitamins A and E, as well as beta carotene, potassium, and calcium.

This nutritional aspect, along with their great flavor, makes them both good choices for baby's first food. Sweet potatoes go well with rice cereal, apples, peaches, pears, carrots, green beans, parsnip, peas, pumpkin, rice, chicken, beef, pork, and yogurt.

Sweet potatoes can be boiled, micro-waved, or baked. If boiling, peel first, cut into large chunks and boil in a sauce pan for about 20 to 30 minutes. Check the tenderness prior to removing from the stove. You might keep the cooking water if you plan to use the potatoes for pureeing.

If you choose to microwave, wrap each sweet potato in cellophane and poke holes in the plastic wrap all around the potato. Cook on a high setting for 10 minutes or until done. If baking, place in the oven at 400 degrees and cook for one hour. Turn over halfway through the cooking time. Thus, if planning to bake your sweet potatoes, allow yourself extra time.

Sweet potatoes are a favorite of most children and they can be spiced up with a number of other foods that make for an excellent taste. When my middle child was having a "picky day," I'd pull out the sweet potatoes and she'd come right out of it!

Sweet Potato Puree

Ingredients:

1 sweet potato

Cook potato using one of the previously described methods. Once cooked, scoop out the potato and put into a food processor or blender. You can add a little breast milk or the cooking liquid to keep the mixture from drying out. Puree until you achieve the desired texture and serve immediately.

Scalloped Sweet Potatoes

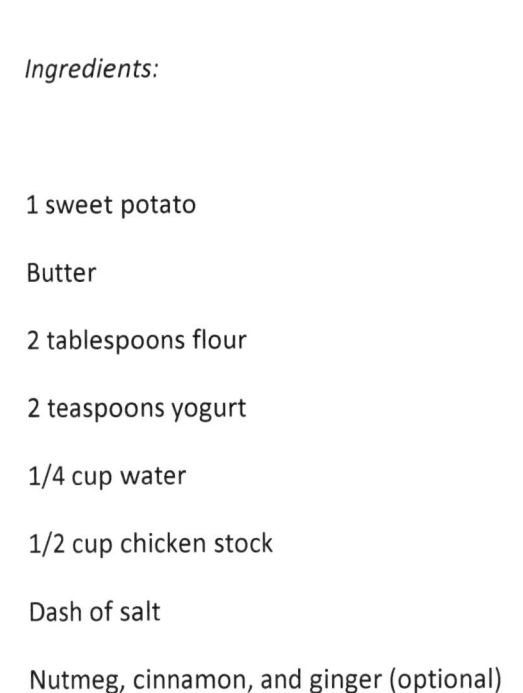

Ingredients:

1 sweet potato

Butter

2 tablespoons flour

2 teaspoons yogurt

1/4 cup water

1/2 cup chicken stock

Dash of salt

Nutmeg, cinnamon, and ginger (optional)

Clean, peel, and slice your potato into very thin slices. Grease a small baking dish with butter. Next, layer the potatoes in the baking dish. In a medium sauce pan, prepare the sauce. Start by melting the butter and then stir in the flour until mixed well. Slowly add the broth, then the yogurt, and then the salt. Cook for 10 to 15 minutes or until the sauce gets thick and bubbly. Stir continuously to avoid burning the sauce. Pour the sauce mixture over the potatoes in the baking dish. Distribute evenly. If you wish, sprinkle the cinnamon or nutmeg over the top of this dish. Bake at 400 degrees for about an hour. Check the tenderness of the potatoes prior to taking them out of the oven. Mash the potatoes with the back of a fork. You can multiply the ingredients in this recipe to make a nice side dish for the entire family.

Sweet Potato Apple Mash

Two of the greats that every child loves! You'll find this combination of apples and sweet potatoes a winning combination!

Ingredients:

1 apple

1 sweet potato

Peel, core, and dice the apples into cubes. Peel, clean, and cube the sweet potato. Place apples and sweet potato in a steamer basket in a medium sauce pan, filled with three inches of water. Cook until tender. Remove from pot and place in a blender or food processor and puree until desired texture is achieved.

Sweet Potatoes and Squash

Ingredients:

1 sweet potato

1 small acorn squash

Peel and clean the sweet potato and cut into small cubes. Peel the squash and cut into small cubes. Add cubes to a steamer basket and place in a medium sized sauce pan, filled with about three inches of water. Steam until the potato and squash are both tender. Remove from the steamer basket and put in a blender or food processor. You can add breast milk or water to moisten the mixture. Puree until you achieve desired texture.

Peachy Yam Bake

Ingredients:

2 cups mashed sweet potatoes

1 cup fresh mashed peaches

1 1/2 tablespoons flour

1 tablespoon butter

1/4 teaspoon nutmeg

1/4 teaspoon cinnamon

1 teaspoon brown sugar

Combine sugar (optional), flour, and spices. Mix in the butter until the ingredients become crumbly. Arrange sweet potatoes and peaches in medium baking pan, sprinkle with butter mixture. Bake at 350 degrees for 35 minutes. Mash this mixture with the back of a fork.

Roasted Sweet Potatoes

Even my husband loves this when I make it for my little ones!

Ingredients:

1 sweet potato

Olive oil

Dash of salt and pepper

Maple syrup (optional)

Preheat oven to 400 degrees. Peel the sweet potato and cut into thin stick-like pieces (think French fries). Place in a medium bowl and drizzle with olive oil. Add just a dash of salt and pepper. Place the sweet potatoes on a baking sheet and cook in the oven for 18 to 20 minutes. Coat with maple syrup (optional).

Peas

Peas have a very high nutritional value, which is amazing for such a small vegetable. Some essential nutrients found in peas include calcium, vitamins A and C, and minerals like iron. One cup of peas contains more protein that a spoonful of peanut butter. Peas are one of the first green vegetables that baby can eat and most babies seem to like them.

Select fresh peas that have not been shelled. Buy them close to the time that you plan to use them, as they don't have a long shelf life. The pods should feel like velvet in your hands. Don't pick pods that feel overly thick or tough, as these may be over-ripe. Also avoid droopy or blackened pods, as these may not be fresh enough. You want the peas to be firm and crisp with a nice green color. Try to buy medium-sized pods rather than large ones.

Start by shelling your peas. This involves opening the pods and taking the peas out. Place the shelled peas into a bowl until you're ready to steam. Put the peas into your steamer basket with enough water that you can just see it coming up through the bottom of the steamer basket. Watch the water level as you cook to avoid burning your pan. Steam the peas until they feel tender.

Pour the steamed peas into an ice-cold bowl of water. This helps create a smoother puree. Place the peas into your mixing bowl, blender, or food processor and use the puree setting. Use your leftover water to add to the puree if you so choose. If you feel that there is too much skin, you can try pouring your puree through the sieve to make it smoother. Peas can be served with apples, carrots, potato, sweet potato, brown rice, chicken, beef, and pork.

Peas can be a lot of fun and are considered by many kids to be one of those "silly" foods. As my oldest giggles, "They pop in my mouth." As a mom, I was unaware of the enjoyment peas could bring, but you'll find that by preparing the right recipes, you'll likely get a lot of thank you's!

Creamed Peas

Ingredients:

3 cups peas, fresh

3/4 cup milk

1½ tablespoons flour

1½ tablespoons butter

Salt and pepper to taste

Place a medium saucepan on the stove over medium heat and melt butter until liquefied. Slowly add flower and mix together well. Add the milk slowly again, mixing as it is added. Try to smash any lumps that appear. Add salt and pepper to taste (optional). Let set until sauce thickens, add the peas, and cook for six minutes. Serve with rice or other meats.

Peas with Mint and Rice

Ingredients:

1 cup uncooked rice

1 3/4 cups homemade chicken stock

1½ cup frozen peas

1/4 cup minced scallions

1/4 cup chopped fresh mint

In a medium saucepan, bring the chicken broth to a boil. Pour in the rice - cover and simmer for 15 minutes. Add the peas and cook for another 5 minutes. Let rice set for 2 - 4 minutes prior to serving.

Zesty Peas, Cauliflower, and Tofu

This recipe is so delicious and tasty. The coconut and soy sauce seem to add a unique taste that hits the spot!

Ingredients:

1 cup fresh peas

1 cup fresh cauliflower

1/2 lb. tofu, firm, cubed

1/2 onion, medium size

1 tablespoon garlic, minced

1/3 cup coconut, unsweetened shredded

12 ounces of pulp-free orange juice

1 orange, peeled, sectioned, and cut in half

1 teaspoon ginger, ground

1/4 teaspoon turmeric, powder

Pepper to taste

1½ soy sauce (low sodium)

1/2 tablespoon cornstarch

In a medium saucepan, place peeled and diced onion and garlic. Cook until they both look clear or translucent. Stir frequently. Add remaining ingredients and mix well until heated through. Add the orange sections and the coconut; continue to cook for five more minutes. In a separate bowl, mix the soy sauce and the sauce, then stir until all of the lumps are gone. Mix until thick and then pour over the fruit and vegetables. Serve over rice.

Peas and Pasta Shells with Parmesan

Ingredients:

1/4 cup fresh peas

1 - 2 tablespoons Parmesan cheese

1 tablespoon butter

1/2 cup pasta shells

In a medium saucepan, boil the pasta shells on medium to high heat. Cook for six minutes and then add the peas. Cook for two more minutes. Drain pasta and peas and place in a medium bowl. Add the butter and cheese, mix well. You can serve as is or puree to desired texture.

Spanish Rice with Peas

Little ones find peas so much fun! My youngest use to giggle every time they "popped" in her mouth!

Ingredients:

1 cup uncooked rice

1/4 Spanish onion

2 tablespoons tomato sauce

1½ cup chicken stock

1/2 teaspoon cooking oil

1/2 cup fresh peas

In a medium pan, pour the oil and heat on medium. Add the onion and the rice, sauté until clear. Add the tomato sauce and stir well. Slowly add the chicken stock and bring to a boil. Cover and let simmer for 23 minutes. Add the peas and simmer for another seven minutes. Serve with rice, beans, shredded cheese, and cut up tortillas.

Breakfast

From the time my kids were babies, breakfast has been one of the most enjoyable meals of the day. I think one of the best things you can do for your child is to start the day off with a healthy breakfast.

Breakfast is the most important meal of the day from the time they can first eat food to the time they can no longer eat! Giving your child a healthy and nutritionally balanced breakfast helps start his or her off with the nutrition that he/she needs.

Typical foods for breakfast include those with high protein, high fiber, and carbohydrates such as whole grain products, fruit, yogurt, oatmeal, and eggs. Using these basic ingredients, you can come up with several varieties of dishes. For example, eggs can be combined with cheese, ham, bacon, or sausage. Fruit can be combined with oatmeal, rice cereal, or yogurt. Toast can be combined with cheese, meat, and other spreads. Bagels are a yummy and chewy treat for your baby.

Brown Rice Cereal

Ingredients:

2 ounces brown rice powder

8 fluid ounces water

A splash of formula or breast milk

Put the water on the stove to boil. While you wait, pour the rice in a blender and grind until it has turned into a powdery texture. When the water is boiling, add the rice powder, stirring constantly with a wire whisk. Turn the heat down to simmer and continue to stir for 10 minutes. Add formula or breast milk to give the desired consistency. Serve with fruit puree.

Apple, Pumpkin, and Oatmeal Breakfast Baby Food Recipe

Ingredients:

1/2 cup applesauce

1/2 cup pumpkin puree

1½ cup (cooked) oatmeal

Dash of cinnamon

Mix applesauce, pumpkin puree, and oatmeal together. Add breast milk if needed for thinning.

Blueberry Muffins (Over 1 year Old)

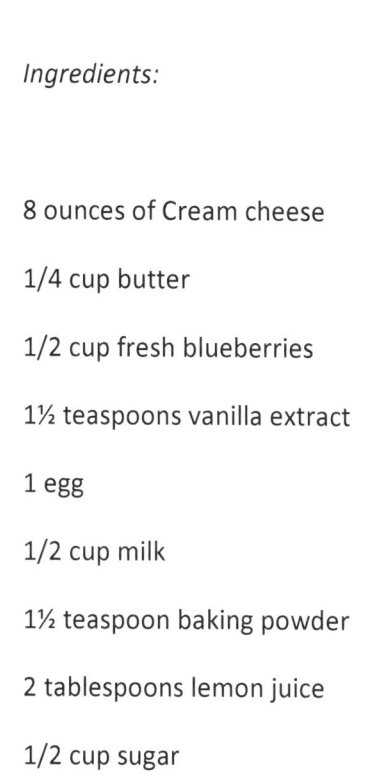

Ingredients:

8 ounces of Cream cheese

1/4 cup butter

1/2 cup fresh blueberries

1½ teaspoons vanilla extract

1 egg

1/2 cup milk

1½ teaspoon baking powder

2 tablespoons lemon juice

1/2 cup sugar

1 cup flour

Preheat the oven to 350 degrees. Rinse blueberries and set aside. Prepare muffin pans with cupcake liners. In a large bowl, combine the Cream cheese, butter, lemon juice, vanilla, and sugar. You can use an electric mixer or a fork. Mix until smooth. Add milk, egg, flour, and baking powder. Mix together well and then add in the blueberries. Bake for 20 to 24 minutes or until golden brown. Poke with a knife to ensure muffins are cooked all the way through. If the knife comes out clean, the muffin is cooked. You can also substitute cranberries for the blueberries.

Oatmeal with Apricots (9 months)

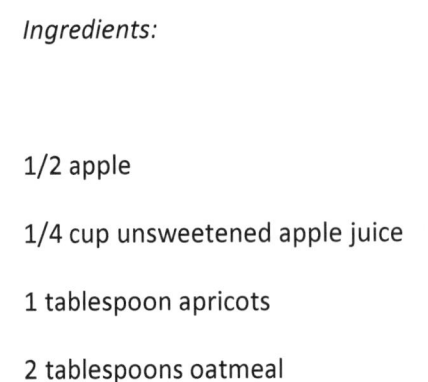

Ingredients:

1/2 apple

1/4 cup unsweetened apple juice

1 tablespoon apricots

2 tablespoons oatmeal

Peel, rinse and core the apple. Cut the apple into small pieces and place in food processor. Add the apple juice and cooked oatmeal. Puree until desired texture is reached.

Cheesy Eggs and Ham (9 months)

Ingredients:

2 egg yolks

1 tablespoon milk

1 tablespoon butter

2 tablespoons grated cheese

2 tablespoons ham chopped finely

In a bowl, mix the egg yolk, milk, cheese, and ham. Heat a sauté pan to medium and melt the butter. Pour the egg mixture into the pan and cook for three minutes or until the egg is solid.

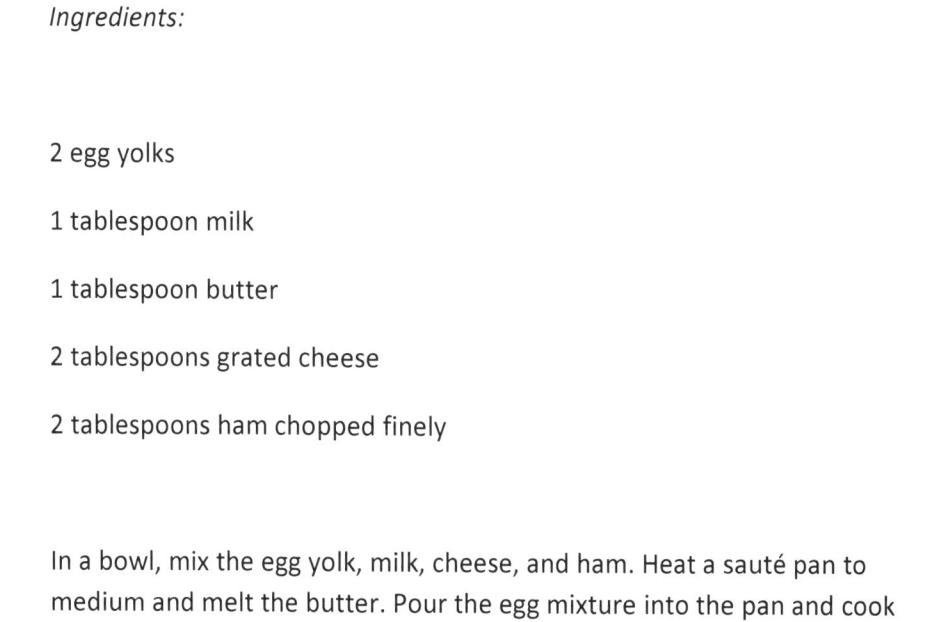

Chile Quiles (Over one year old)

Ingredients:

4 corn tortillas

4 thin slices of Spanish onion

1½ teaspoons vegetable oil

2 tablespoons tomato sauce

Salt and pepper to taste

2 tablespoons grated cheese

Cut the tortillas into 8 triangular sections. Heat a sauté pan on medium heat and add the oil and onion. Stir for one minute and then add the tortillas. Mix well. Pour the tomato sauce evenly over the tortillas. Add a dash of salt and pepper. Continue to stir until completely cooked through. Top with cheese. Puree if you like or serve as is. Serve with scrambled eggs and/or refried beans. This is a meal that your entire family will like and it's easy to multiply the ingredients to make more for everyone.

French toast Dippers (Over one year)

This is one of the greatest fun food recipes that your kids will devour, no matter what their age! My kids request French toast dippers at least once a week.

Ingredients:

1 slice of bread (whole wheat or sourdough)

1 egg

1/4 cup milk

Two drops of vanilla

Cinnamon

Heat a pan or griddle to medium and spray with a non-stick spray or grease with butter. In a small bowl, mix the egg, milk, vanilla, and cinnamon. Dip the bread into the egg mixture and fully cover. Place dipped bread in the pan and heat until golden brown, then turn and heat the other side until golden brown. Remove cooked French toast and cut into strips. Serve with maple syrup so that the French toast can be dipped into the syrup. You can also add fresh berries or scrambled egg on the side.

Roast Beef Hash

I remember when my children first started to eat their first tastes of meat. It was such a special, joyful time. When you begin to introduce meat, the smiles on your child's face will seem to last forever! With each of mine, it was truly a special time that I'll always remember.

Ingredients:

1 Russet potato

1 slice of roast beef (you can use lunch meat or leftovers)

2 tablespoons butter

1/2 teaspoon chopped onion

Salt and pepper

Clean and peel the potato. Cut into three parts and place in a medium saucepan filled two-thirds full with water. Boil for about 20 minutes or until the potato is softened. Remove the potato from the water and cut into small cubes, then set aside. Remove the fat from the roast beef and cut into cubes, set aside. In a skillet, melt the butter and onion and cook onion until it's clear. Add the potato cubes and the pieces of roast beef. Mix well with the butter and cook until golden brown.

Crushed Cheerios in Banana Puree

Ingredients:

1/2 cup plain Cheerios

1 banana

Breast milk

Slice the bananas and place in a food processor. Add the Cheerios and a splash of breast milk. Puree until the desire texture is reached. Serve immediately.

Eggs with Tomatoes and Cheese

If tomatoes are a new food, then definitely make sure that you use the four-day test to ensure your child does not have any reactions or digestive problems with it.

Ingredients:

2 eggs

1 tablespoon milk

1 tablespoon butter

2 tablespoons grated Cheddar cheese

1/2 tablespoon chopped tomato

Place the butter in a sauté pan and heat to medium. In a bowl, whisk together the eggs, milk, and cheese. Add the egg mixture to the sauté pan and cook for about 2 - 3 minutes. Top with the tomato and serve immediately.

Sausage, Egg, and Cheese

For a special Sunday breakfast, this is one that I serve to my kids and husband on a croissant!

Ingredients:

2 breakfast sausage links

1 egg

1/4 cup grated Cheddar cheese

Salt and pepper to taste

Cook the sausage in a pan until brown on all sides. Remove and cut into small pieces. Place in a mixing bowl and add the egg, salt, and pepper. Whisk the egg vigorously. Pour the egg into a preheated greased pan and continue to scramble. Cook all the way through. Serve with toast or biscuit.

Orange Zucchini Muffins (12 months)

Ingredients:

1½ cups of whole wheat flour

1/2 cup flour

1 cup oat bran

2 eggs

1½ cup shredded zucchini

1 teaspoon baking powder

1 teaspoon ground cinnamon

1/2 teaspoon kosher salt

¼ teaspoon baking soda

1/3 cup canola oil

3/4 cup brown sugar

1/4 cup sugar

1/3 cup organic orange juice

Preheat the oven to 350 degrees. Prepare muffin pans with cooking spray or cupcake liners. In a medium bowl, mix the eggs, oil, juice, and the sugar - mix well. Add the zucchini and mix well. Slowly add the baking powder, baking soda, oat bran, flour, cinnamon, and salt. Combine until ingredients are thoroughly mixed. Add mixture to muffin pans with a spoon or small measuring cup. Bake for 24 minutes. Check to ensure that the muffins are baked all the way through by using a knife or a toothpick. It should come out clean. Muffins are now ready to eat!

Sweet Potato Pancakes

Ingredients:

2 cups of white whole wheat flour

2 large eggs

3 teaspoon baking powder

1/2 teaspoon kosher salt

1 teaspoon ground cinnamon

1 large sweet potato

2 cups milk

1/4 cup melted butter

3 tablespoon brown sugar

1 tablespoon vanilla extract

Preheat the griddle to medium heat. Coat the pan with butter or cooking spray. Peel, clean, and cut the sweet potato into small chunks. Place in the blender and puree until smooth. Set aside. In a large mixing bowl, add the flour, baking powder, salt, cinnamon, and sugar. Add the eggs, milk, butter, vanilla, and sweet potato. Mix together well. Pour about ¼ cup of batter onto the pan and watch for air bubbles to disappear. Flip and do the same for the other side.

Chicken

Chicken is a very versatile and easy food to serve, not to mention affordable. Children normally love it. You can boil, grill, or bake a chicken breast and then puree it with other ingredients such as apples or rice. You can prepare a whole chicken for your family and just cut off some pieces to serve to your baby - so easy!

Chicken is one of the healthier meats, as it is low in fat and high in protein. Many people opt to buy organically raised chicken to avoid the antibiotics and other hormones that might be found in chicken sold in supermarkets.

When cooking chicken or turkey, always make certain to cook completely and to wash your hands after touching the poultry. This reduces the chance of contacting or cross-contaminating with salmonella, which is found on raw chicken and eggs. Many people opt to use ground turkey in place of other ground meats. In this section, you'll notice a recipe for turkey chili, which is a very mild dish that toddlers love to eat. Ground turkey can also be used for turkey burgers when barbecuing.

Chicken, Rice, and Applesauce

This is the idea recipe for young ones that have just started eating solids.

Ingredients:

1/4 cup chicken

1 clove of garlic

1/2 cup brown rice uncooked

1/2 cup orzo

2 cups chicken stock

2 tablespoons butter

2 shallots finely minced (you can also leave the shallots in big chunks that can be taken out when you are ready to serve)

Pepper to taste (optional)

2 tablespoons apple puree

Prepare the rice as follows. In a medium sauce pan, melt the butter and add the shallots, rice, and orzo. Continue to stir until the ingredients become clear. Slowly add stock and bring to a boil. Cover the pan and cook for 25 minutes.

While the rice is cooking, boil one chicken breast in water with garlic, salt, and pepper. Cook chicken for 25 minutes and then set aside. Save the broth to use for future recipes. Use about one quarter of the chicken and refrigerate or freeze the rest. Either cut this into very small pieces or grind the meat in a food processor or blender. Prepare about one-half cup of rice, add the chicken, and add the apple puree. Mix well and serve.

Mixed Chicken and Vegetables

This is such a simple recipe and one that always amazes me when I see the excitement on my children's faces when I serve it. It's a great tasting recipe that's also bright, colorful, and nutritious!

Ingredients:

1/4 cup chicken breast

1 carrot

1/4 cup peas

Homemade chicken stock

In a medium sauce pan, place the chicken stock, chicken breast, carrots, and peas. Cook on medium high heat for 20 minutes. Remove the chicken, set aside to cool and then shred into bite size pieces. Set the cooking water aside. Place the chicken, carrots, and peas in a bowl, mix with a hand mixer. If too dry, add a little of the cooking broth until desired consistency is reached.

Creamed Peas and Chicken

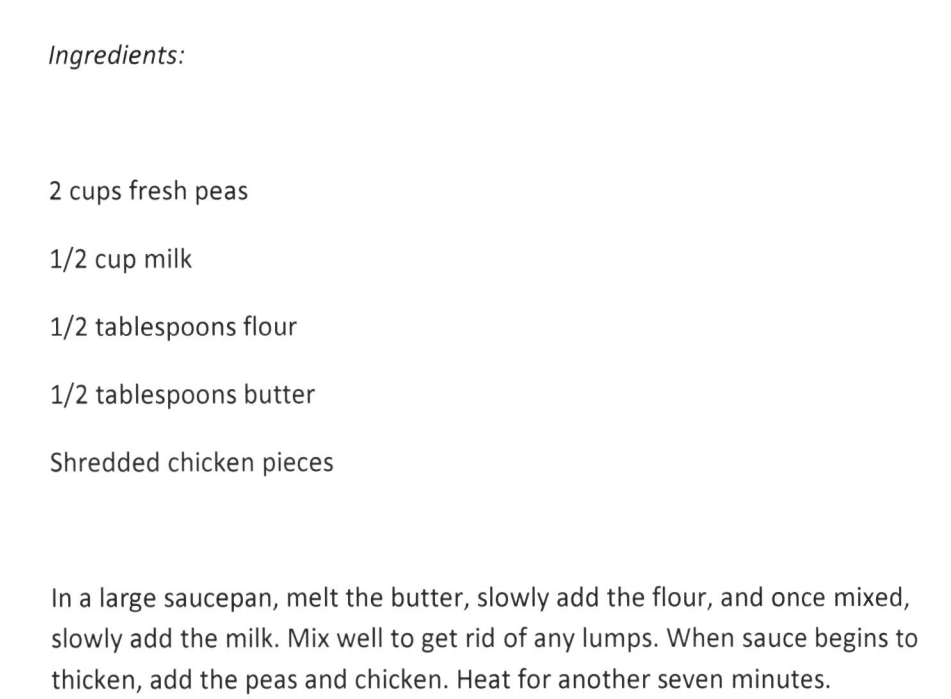

Ingredients:

2 cups fresh peas

1/2 cup milk

1/2 tablespoons flour

1/2 tablespoons butter

Shredded chicken pieces

In a large saucepan, melt the butter, slowly add the flour, and once mixed, slowly add the milk. Mix well to get rid of any lumps. When sauce begins to thicken, add the peas and chicken. Heat for another seven minutes.

Chicken with Blueberry Sauce and Mint

This is one of the favorites we have when Grandma visits! The kids always tell "Nana" that they made it especially for her! I think you'll agree. It is a great tasting meal!

Ingredients:

1/2 cup boiled chicken breast

1/4 cup blueberries

1 teaspoon Monterey Jack cheese

1 mint sprig

Grate cheese and set aside. Rinse the blueberries and place them in a food processor. Cut the chicken into small chunks and place in the food processor. Puree until desired texture is reached. Sprinkle the cheese on top. Garnish with mint.

Breaded Chicken

Ingredients:

1 boneless, skinless chicken breast

1/2 cup fresh bread crumbs

1/2 cup Parmesan cheese

1/2 cup milk

Preheat oven to 350 degrees. Clean and trim chicken. Place chicken breast between two pieces of wax paper and gently pound out. Mix the cheese and bread crumbs in a bowl. Dip the chicken in the milk and thoroughly cover with liquid. Remove chicken from milk mixture and roll around in the bread crumb mixture until covered. Place the chicken on a non-stick baking sheet and cook in the oven for 25 minutes. Check to make certain that the chicken is fully cooked. Serve with mashed potatoes or rice. You can multiply this recipe for your entire family. Salt and pepper to taste.

Rice and Chicken

Ingredients:

1 cup uncooked rice

3/4 Spanish onion

2 tablespoons tomato sauce

1½ cups chicken stock

1/2 teaspoon cooking oil

1 boneless skinless chicken breast

1 potato

1/4 cup fresh peas (optional)

Clean the chicken and cut into medium sized chunks. Peel, clean, and cut the potato into small chunks. In a medium pan, pour the oil and heat on medium. Add the onion, rice, and the chicken - sauté for five minutes. Add the tomato sauce and stir well. Slowly add the chicken stock and potatoes and bring to a boil. Cover and let simmer for 30 minutes. Add the peas and cook for another five minutes. Serve with rice, beans, shredded cheese, and cut up tortillas.

Carrots and Turkey

Another easy recipe that is nutritious, tasty, and great for new meat eaters.

Ingredients:

2 ounces of ground turkey

1½ cups of water

1/2 cup rice

1 carrot

1 tablespoon of butter

In a medium saucepan, bring the water to a boil. Add the rice and cover to reduce the heat to simmer. Cook for 20 minutes. In a sauté pan, melt the butter and add the ground turkey. Cook until browned all the way through and then set aside. Clean and chop carrots into wheels. When the rice is done, add the carrot and cook for another five minutes or until carrot are tender. Mix the turkey in with the rice mixture. Serve as is or puree until desired texture is reached.

Chicken, Potato, Cheese, and Rice

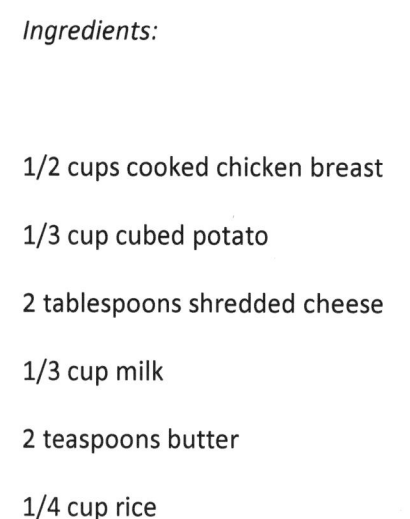

Ingredients:

1/2 cups cooked chicken breast

1/3 cup cubed potato

2 tablespoons shredded cheese

1/3 cup milk

2 teaspoons butter

1/4 cup rice

In a medium sauce pan, mix the chicken, milk, butter, and potato. Turn on low heat and cook for 10 minutes. Add the cheese and mix well. Add the rice and mix together well. Either serves as is or puree until desired texture is reached.

Turkey Chili

Ingredients:

1/2 pound ground turkey

1 teaspoon olive oil

1 cup of canned kidney beans

1½ cups fresh tomato crushed

1/2 cup onions chopped

1/2 tablespoon minced garlic

1 tablespoon chili powder (optional to taste)

1/4 teaspoon paprika

1/4 teaspoon cayenne pepper

1/4 teaspoon oregano

1/4 teaspoon cumin

Salt and pepper to taste

In a medium pot, add the olive oil and turkey and cook until brown on all sides. Add the onion and cook for 2-3 minutes. Add the water, tomatoes, and garlic. Drain and rinse the kidney beans, add to the pot. Add the rest of the seasonings and bring the mixture to a boil. Cover and reduce heat to simmer. Cook for at least 30 minutes. Stir occasionally. Serve with cornbread or toast.

Soup

Soup is a great meal for those cold days, as it warms you and your baby up. Soup is a good way to serve grains, meats, and vegetables in a yummy, flavorful broth. Soup is also great for those times when baby has been feeling a little under the weather, especially if he/she has a sore throat or upset tummy.

Basic soup recipes can be adapted by adding vegetables, rice, and meat. Soup tends to be made in large quantities and it saves well so you can make some today and warm up the leftovers tomorrow. Give yourself a minimum of 30 minutes when making soup in order to allow enough time for the broth to boil and the ingredients to cook through and soften.

Mama's Special Soup (Over one year)

I love when I hear my kids refer to this soup as "Mama's Special Soup." Little names like that are things that kids carry with them their entire life. I remember my mom used to have what she called "Mama Fries" and when she made them, we always felt like there was something special in the house.

Ingredients:

1 cup star shaped pasta

1/4 Spanish onion

1 tablespoon vegetable oil

4 ounces tomato sauce

3 - 4 cups of homemade chicken stock

Cut one quarter chunk out of the onion, peel, and core. Place in a medium saucepan with 1 tablespoon of oil. Add the star-shaped pasta and sauté on medium heat for about 3-4 minutes until the pasta and the onions turn clear. Be sure to keep stirring to avoid burning. Add four ounces of tomato sauce, stir for a minute, and then immediately add the chicken stock. Bring to a boil and then simmer for at least 20 minutes. Serve with lemon. You can change the pasta used for this soup. The stars were chosen due to their small size, which makes them easy to chew. Small pasta shells also work great for this soup.

Sweet Potato Soup

Ingredients:

2 large sweet potatoes

2 cups homemade chicken stock

1/2 cup celery diced

1/4 cup diced onion

1 tablespoon vegetable oil

1 bay leaf

1/4 teaspoon basil

In a medium saucepan, add the vegetable oil and heat to medium. Sauté the onion and celery until clear. Add the potatoes, chicken stock, basil, and bay leaf. Bring to a boil and reduce heat to simmer. Cook for 30 minutes. Remove the bay leaf and pour the mixture into a food processor or blender. Blend until smooth and serve.

Squash and Rice Soup

Ingredients:

1 cup cooked mashed butternut squash (works well with pumpkin too)

1/2 cup water

1/4 cup cooked brown rice

Dollop yogurt

Mash squash with the water in a food processor or blender and slowly mix in the brown rice. Process to a consistency that your baby enjoys and can handle. Once you have the desired consistency, add the yogurt and stir.

Sweet Potato Soup (8 months)

Ingredients:

1½ cups cooked sweet potatoes

1 tablespoon flour

1 tablespoon butter

1½ cups chicken broth

1 tablespoon light brown sugar

1/4 teaspoon ground ginger

1/8 teaspoon ground cinnamon

1/8 teaspoon ground nutmeg

1 cup milk

In a large saucepan, melt the butter. Once melted, slowly add the flour until mixed together. Add the broth and brown sugar, bring to a boil. Slowly add the sweet potatoes, stirring constantly. Turn the heat down to simmer and cook for another eight minutes. Pour one-third of the soup into the blender and puree, set aside. Repeat this step until all of the soup is pureed and then pour the soup back into the pot. Add the milk and heat for another 10 minutes. Add salt and pepper to taste.

Lemony Chicken and Rice Soup

Ingredients:

1 cup of white rice

1 teaspoon cooking oil

1/4 onion minced finely

3 cups of homemade chicken stalk

1 boneless, skinless chicken breast

1 lemon

2 tablespoons cream

Salt and pepper

1 clove of garlic

Fill a medium sauce pan 3½ cups of water. Add chicken breast, salt, pepper, and the clove of garlic (cut in half). Cook chicken breast for 20 minutes. Remove chicken and set aside. Run the broth through a strainer to remove particles. In the same saucepan, add the cooking oil, sauté the onion, and the rice until the onion is clear. Squeeze the lemon juice into the pot and mix well. Slowly, add the broth that was set aside. Cut the chicken breast into small bites and add it to the soup mixture. Cook for at least 20 minutes or until the rice is softened. After 20 minutes, slowly add the cream to thicken the mixture. Serve as is or puree to desired texture.

Cold Vegetable Soup

Ingredients:

6 cherry tomatoes

1/2 cup raw spinach

1 stick of celery

1/2 avocado

1 lemon

Salt and pepper to taste

Clean the tomatoes and remove the tops. Clean the spinach and remove any darkened pieces. Clean the celery and remove any strings. Cut the avocado in half and remove the seed. Use a juicer to squeeze the juice out of the lemon. Avoid getting seeds in the juice. Add all of the ingredients to a food processor or blender. Blend well and puree to desired texture. Add salt and pepper to taste. Serve cold with a dollop of sour cream.

Cream of Pumpkin Soup

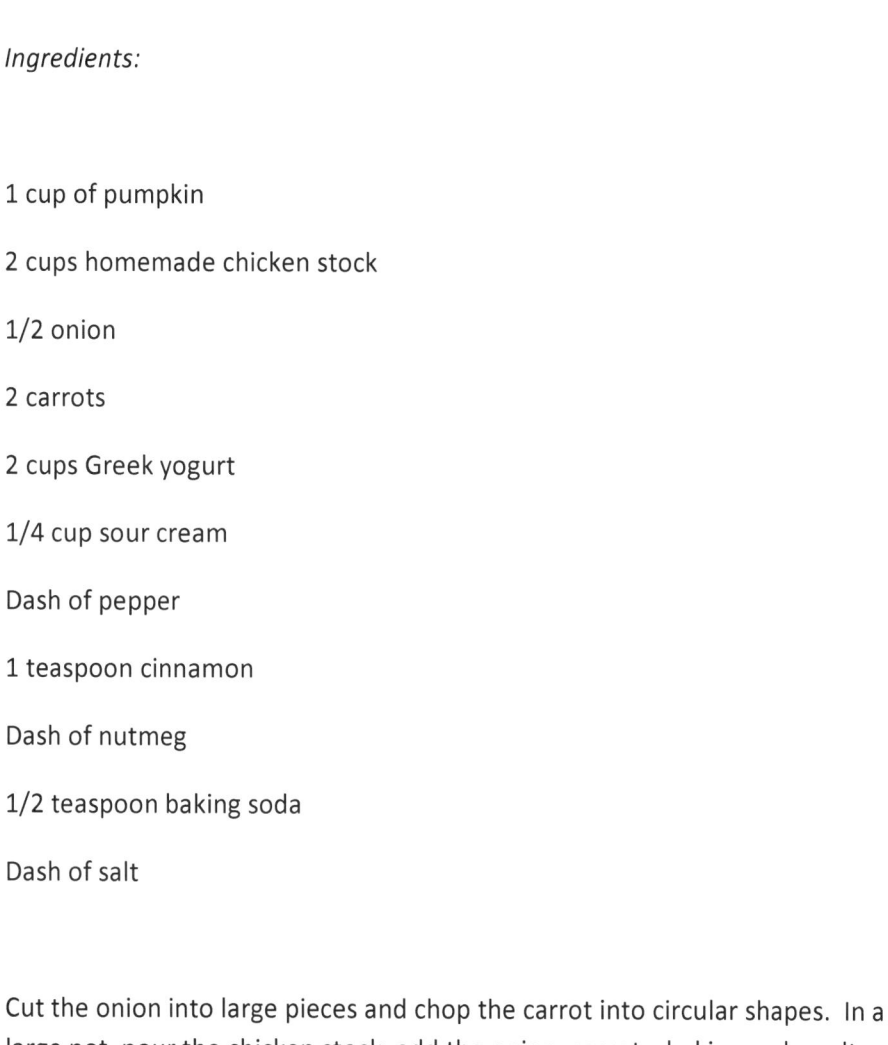

Ingredients:

1 cup of pumpkin

2 cups homemade chicken stock

1/2 onion

2 carrots

2 cups Greek yogurt

1/4 cup sour cream

Dash of pepper

1 teaspoon cinnamon

Dash of nutmeg

1/2 teaspoon baking soda

Dash of salt

Cut the onion into large pieces and chop the carrot into circular shapes. In a large pot, pour the chicken stock, add the onion, carrots, baking soda, salt, and pepper. Cook for 15 minutes or until the carrots have softened. Add the pumpkin and yogurt - cook uncovered on low heat for fifteen minutes. You can puree this for younger kids or serve as is. Add a dollop of sour cream.

Squash Soup (8 months)

When your baby is old enough definitely introduce this soup - it's sure to be a hit!

Ingredients:

1½ pounds winter squash

1/2 onion

1 teaspoon curry powder

1/4 teaspoon ground turmeric

2 cups chicken broth

1/2 teaspoon cooking oil

Dash of salt and pepper

Cut the squash into cubes. In a medium sauce pan, sauté the onions until clear. Add the squash and spices. Simmer on low heat for 15 minutes. Pour in the broth and cook for another 15 minutes. Pour the soup into a blender or food processor and blend until desired texture is reached. Serve with sour cream.

Apples

Apples are another one of those wonder foods. Every day, we hear more and more health benefits associated with eating them. Apples have several vitamins and minerals. They are also a great source of fiber, which can aid with digestion. They contain anti-oxidants, which help protect the brain and have even been associated with reducing the development of lung and breast cancer.

Apples are a good source of carbohydrates and can provide a quick energy boost. You can choose from several different types of apples, though the three most popular apples include McIntosh, Granny Smith, and Gala. As your kids grow older, you can serve slices of apple with cheese and crackers. This is a great snack. For babies, you will want to puree the apples into an applesauce mixture, maybe adding a little cinnamon. Applesauce is generally a very popular food amongst children and it goes well with meat, chicken, and pork.

We couldn't live without applesauce in our home! My little ones enjoy it with dinners, as a snack, and as a dessert. It's a menu item that is affordable, tasty, and nutritious so allow your children lots of opportunities to enjoy this wonderful fruit!

Applesauce

Ingredients:

5 apples, peeled, cored, and cut into cubes

Breast milk

Rice cereal

Cinnamon stick (optional)

Into a medium saucepan, add about three inches of water and then place a steamer basket in the pan. Add the cubed apple to the steamer basket. You can also add a cinnamon stick if you choose. Steam the apples until tender, around eight minutes. Drain the water, remove the cinnamon stick, and place the apples in a blender or food processor. Puree until desired texture is achieved. Chill and serve cold.

Apple Zing Puree

Ingredients:

3 medium apples

1/2 red onion

1 tablespoon olive oil

Salt and pepper

Preheat the oven to 350 degrees. Peel, core, and cut apples into large chunks. Slice the onion into one-inch slices. Put the apples and onions into a medium mixing bowl; add the olive oil and a dash of salt. Place the apples and the onions on a baking sheet and cook for about 22 minutes or until tender.

Apples and Yogurt

Ingredients:

3 tablespoons apple puree

2 tablespoons Greek yogurt

Mix the apple puree and the yogurt together. Serve cold with cereal.

Pear and Apple Puree

Ingredients:

1 apple

1 pear

Water

Into a medium sauce pan, add about three inches of water. Place a steamer basket in the pan and turn on to boil. Peel, core, and rinse both the apple and the pear. Slice into thin slices and place slices in the steamer basket. Cover with a lid and steam the fruit for nine minutes or until tender. Remove the fruit from the steamer basket and place in a blender or food processor. Puree until desired texture is reached. You can add breast milk if the mixture is too dry.

Apple Grahams Delight

Ingredients:

1 apple

1 graham cracker

Into a medium saucepan, add about three inches of water. Peel, core, and slice the apple. Place the sliced apples in the steamer basket. Bring the water to a boil and steam the apple for eight to nine minutes. While the apple is steaming, crush the graham cracker into very small pieces. Once the apples are steamed, move them to a food processor or blender. Add the crushed graham crackers and a splash of water. Puree until desired texture is reached.

Sweet Cinnamon Apples

Ingredients:

4 large apples

1/2 cup water

1/4 teaspoon cinnamon

1/2 teaspoon vanilla

Fill a medium saucepan about two thirds full with water and heat to medium. Peel, core, and cut apples into small chunks and place in the pot of water. Add the cinnamon and vanilla and cook for about nine minutes or until the fruit is tender. Remove cooked fruit from the pot and put into a blender or food processor, set cooking water aside. Blend until desired texture is reached.

Rice

Rice with Apple and Butternut Squash

Ingredients:

1 Butternut squash

2 cups cooked brown rice

1/2 cup applesauce

Preheat oven to 400 degrees. Cut squash in half and scoop out the seeds. Place the squash halves face down in a medium baking dish with one to two inches of water. Place in the oven and cook for 45 minutes or until the skin becomes puckered. Scoop the squash out of the shell and put in blender or food processor. Add the cooked rice and the applesauce to the blender or food processor, puree until desired texture is reached. Add water as necessary to achieve a smooth, thin consistency.

Rice Pilaf

Ingredients:

1/2 cup brown rice uncooked

1/2 cup orzo

2 cups chicken stock

2 tablespoons butter

2 shallots finely minced (you can leave the shallots in big chunks that can be taken out when you are ready to serve)

Pepper to taste (optional)

In a medium sauce pan, melt the butter; add the shallots, rice, and orzo. Continue to stir until the ingredients become clear. Slowly add stock and bring to a boil. Cover pan and cook for 25 minutes. Serve with a main dish such as chicken or beef.

Spanish Rice

Ingredients:

1 cup uncooked rice

1/4 Spanish onion

2 tablespoons tomato sauce

1½ cup chicken stock

1/2 teaspoon cooking oil

Into a medium pan, pour oil and heat on medium. Add the onion and the rice and sauté until clear. Add the tomato sauce and stir well. Slowly add the chicken stock and bring to a boil. Cover and let simmer for 30 minutes. Serve with rice, beans, shredded cheese, and cut up tortillas.

Fried Rice

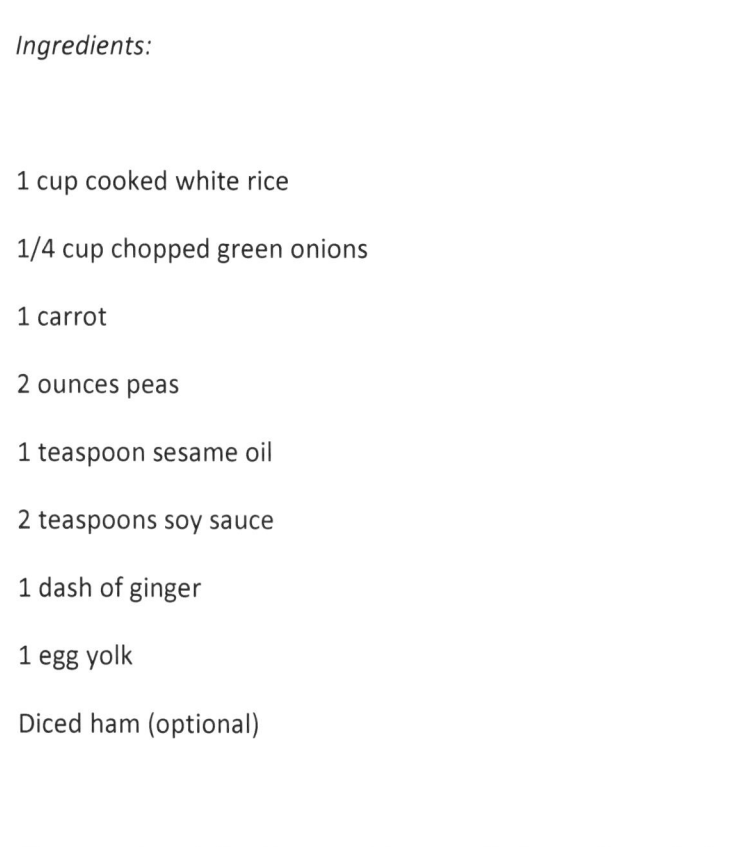

Ingredients:

1 cup cooked white rice

1/4 cup chopped green onions

1 carrot

2 ounces peas

1 teaspoon sesame oil

2 teaspoons soy sauce

1 dash of ginger

1 egg yolk

Diced ham (optional)

Clean, peel, and dice the carrot into small pieces. Heat a frying pan or wok on high. Add the sesame oil, carrots, and onions. Add the rice, egg, peas, and ham. Mix well. Add the soy sauce and ginger. Mix for three to four minutes or until all of the ingredients are heated through. Serve immediately.

Cheesy Rice with Bacon Bits

Ingredients:

1/2 cup Arborio rice

1/4 cup cooked bacon, diced

1½ cups of chicken stock

2 tablespoons butter

2 tablespoons diced onions

1 clove of garlic, minced

2 tablespoons Parmesan cheese

Salt and pepper to taste

Bring the chicken stock to a boil, then to simmer, and set aside. Cook the bacon until browned, remove from the pan, and set aside. In a medium sauce pan, melt one tablespoon of butter - sauté the onions and the garlic in the butter for about two minutes. Add the rice and continue to stir until the rice turns color. Reduce heat to medium, slowly add about one-third of the chicken stock. Stir until the mixture becomes creamy, add another portion of the stock, and continue to stir. Adding the broth will take about fifteen minutes.

At the end of this time, the rice should be somewhat tender, but not mushy. During this time, dice the bacon into small pieces. Remove the rice from the stove and stir in the last tablespoon of butter, the Parmesan cheese, and the diced bacon. Add salt and pepper to taste. Serve with chicken, beef, or fish.

Cheesy Rice with Lemon

Ingredients:

1/2 cup rice

1¼ cups homemade chicken stock

1/2 leek, sliced thinly

1 tablespoon fresh chives

1/3 cup shredded Mozzarella cheese

2 slices of lemon

Salt and pepper to taste

In a medium saucepan, mix two tablespoons of the chicken stock and the sliced leek - bring to a boil. Cook for about five minutes until the leek is tender. Add the remaining chicken stock and the rice and bring to a boil. Turn the heat down to simmer, place the lid on the pot, and cook for 25 minutes. Stir in the chives and Mozzarella cheese and serve.

Pumpkin Risotto (8 Months)

Ingredients:

1 cup Arborio rice

1/4 cup olive oil

1½ cups homemade chicken stock

1/2 cup onion finely chopped

1/2 tablespoon minced garlic

1/2 cup apple juice

1 cup cubed pumpkin

1/4 cup grated Parmesan

2 tablespoons butter

In a medium size pan, heat the olive oil, sauté the garlic and onion until clear. Add the rice and stir well, cook until clear. Add the apple juice and cook until it is absorbed by the rice. Add the chicken stock in small doses and cook for about 25 minutes. Stir in the pumpkin, cheese, and butter to serve. You can also puree this dish to desired texture for younger babies.

Roast Pumpkin Risotto

Ingredients:

1½ cups of pumpkin

1 cup Arborio Rice

1/2 tablespoon olive oil

2 cups vegetable stock

1/4 teaspoon minced garlic

1/2 onions diced

3 ounces Feta cheese cubed

Salt and pepper to taste

Prepare a medium-size baking dish by rubbing with olive oil. Preheat the oven to 400 degrees. Cut pumpkin open and scoop out the meat. In a medium sauce pan, place three inches of water and insert the steamer basket. Cut the pumpkin into cubes and place them in the basket. Steam for 7 - 9 minutes or until tender.

Remove the pumpkin and place it in the baking dish. Drizzle with olive oil, salt, and pepper. Bake for 15 minutes, then add the cheese to the baking dish, and cook for an additional five minutes. Use a saucepan to sauté the onions, garlic, and rice for 2 -3 minutes. Slowly, add the vegetable stock, stirring frequently. Cook for about 25 minutes and add salt and pepper to taste. Mix the pumpkin with the risotto and add the cubes of Feta. Serve as is or puree until desired thickness is reached.

Sweet Potato Risotto (Over one year)

Ingredients:

2 medium sweet potatoes

1/4 cup olive oil

4 cups vegetable stock

1/2 cup finely chopped onion

1 tablespoon minced garlic

1½ cups Arborio rice

3/4 cup white grape juice

1 tablespoon fresh rosemary

1½ teaspoons thyme leaves

3 tablespoons butter

2 tablespoons grated Parmesan cheese

1 teaspoon salt

3/4 teaspoons black pepper

Preheat oven to 350 degrees. Peel and clean the sweet potatoes. Cut in half. Cut one half of the potato into 1/4 inch cubes. Cut the other half into one-inch chunks. Place both in a bowl and drizzle with olive oil. Mix and cover well. Place in the oven and bake for 30 minutes. Place the cooked, larger chunks of sweet potato in a food processor or blender; add ¼ cup vegetable stock and puree.

Heat a large sauce pan and add 3 tablespoons olive oil. Sauté the onions and the smaller diced sweet potato in the same pot until the onions are clear. Cook the mixture for 3-4 minutes or until softened. Add the garlic and the rice, sauté for another three minutes, stirring constantly. Add the grape juice, constantly stirring.

Repeat this step for the remaining vegetable stock. Add the sweet potato puree, the rosemary, thyme, butter, and Parmesan cheese. Cook on low for ten minutes or until all of the liquid has been absorbed.

In a large saucepan, heat the remaining three tablespoons oil, sauté the onion and the small diced sweet potatoes over medium high heat. Add salt and pepper to taste. Serve with a dollop of sour cream.

Fruit Dishes

In this section, we've included recipes made with a variety of fruits. Fruits are by far "the food" in my home! Since my children were babies, fruit has been an important part of their diet. Since fruits are seasonal, it's best to try to use fruits that are in season, as these will be the ripest and have the most flavor. Depending on where you live, you'll also have a differing variety of fruits available to you. Some of the more tropical fruits such as papaya and mangoes can be found in gourmet food stores.

Farmers' markets tend to offer fruits grown in your local area. The produce at these markets is very fresh and tasty. They are usually sold for lower prices than at a grocery store. Many of these fruits can be finely chopped and combined to make a salsa or chutney, which can be served with chicken, beef, or fish. This makes for a very light and tasty summer meal. I hope you enjoy these tried and true fruit recipes made with love!

Roasted Pears (Over one year)

Ingredients:

1 pear

1/4 teaspoon brown sugar

Preheat oven to 500 degrees. Wash pear, cut in half, and take out the core. Place each pear half face up on a cookie sheet. Sprinkle with brown sugar. Roast in the oven for 25 minutes or until soft. Serve with Greek yogurt. This makes a great desert.

Papaya

Ingredients:

1/2 papaya

1 avocado

4 slices of pineapple

Cut the papaya in half and scoop out the seeds. Cut into small cubes. Cut the avocado in half, remove the seed, and cut into cubes. Cut about four slices of pineapple, remove the core and cut into cubes. Place the cut fruit in a blender or food processor, then puree until desired texture is reached.

Tasty Peaches

Ingredients:

6 peaches

3/4 cup apple juice

Water

Fill a large pot two-thirds full with water, add the apple juice, and place a saucepan on the stove on high heat. Peel, pit, and clean peaches thoroughly. Slice the peaches and place them in the pot of boiling water. Turn the heat down to simmer and cook for 10 to 12 minutes or until peaches are tender. Remove the peaches from the water and put them in a blender or food processor. Puree to desired consistency. Serve warm with cereal or milk. This is a large batch so freeze anything that remains.

Peach Puree

Ingredients:

3 peaches

1 cinnamon sticks (optional over 8 months)

Peal the peaches, rinse, and cut them into slices. Put about three inches of water into a medium sauce pan and place a steamer basket in the same pan. Place peach slices in the steamer. You can also add a cinnamon stick for added flavor if you choose. Steam the peaches for about 6 - 8 minutes or until tender. Remove the cinnamon stick and place the peach slices in a blender or food processor. Puree until desired texture is reached. Serve with Cottage cheese, white rice, or chicken.

Papaya Puree

Ingredients:

1 papaya

Peel papaya and rinse it well. Cut the papaya in half, scoop out the seeds and discard. Cut the papaya into cubes and place in a food processor or blender. Puree until desired texture is reached. Serve with rice, chicken, fish, or bananas.

Kiwi Puree (8 months)

Ingredients:

2 ripe kiwis

Peel and rinse the kiwi, then cut off the ends. Cut into quarters and place into a food processor or blender. Puree until desired texture is reached. Add a splash of water to thin this mixture. Serve cold with Cottage cheese, rice, or cereal.

Kiwi and Banana Surprise

Ingredients:

2 ripe kiwis

1 banana

2 tablespoons water

Peel and rinse kiwi, then cut off the ends. Cut into quarters and place into a food processor or blender. Cut up the bananas and add to food processor. Add 2 tablespoons water. Puree until desired texture is reached. Serve cold with cereal or rice.

Mango Puree (6 months)

Ingredients:

1 mango

Water

Peel and rinse the mango. Cut the mango into cube sized pieces. Cut the mango meat off the seed. Add a splash of water. Puree until desired consistency is reached.

Mango and Banana Puree

Ingredients:

1 mango

1 banana

Peel and rinse the mango. Cut any fruit left on the pit. Place mango in a steamer basket in a medium pot filled with about three inches of water. Steam the mango for six to eight minutes. Remove the mango from the pot and place it in a food processor or blender. Puree for 15 seconds and then add the sliced banana to the mixture. Puree until desired texture is reached. Serve with yogurt.

Banana and Papaya Puree

Ingredients:

1 medium papaya

1 banana

Peel and rinse the papaya. Cut in half and scoop out the seeds. Cut into chunks and place these in a food processor or blender. Slice the banana and place in the food processor or blender. Puree this mixture until desired texture is reached.

Melon

Ingredients:

1/4 honeydew melon

1/4 cucumber

1 tablespoon Cream cheese

Remove the seeds and the rind from the melon and cut into chunks. Clean and peel the cucumber cut into chunks and remove the seeds. Place both the melon and the cucumber into a food processor or blender, then puree. Soften the Cream cheese with a fork. Mix the puree with the Cream cheese and serve immediately.

Strawberries and Creamy Yogurt

Ingredients:

4 fresh strawberries

4 ounces Greek yogurt

Clean the berries and remove the stem and center. Place them in a blender or food processor, then puree for 15 seconds. Pour the mixture through a strainer to remove the seeds. Mix the berry puree into the yogurt in a swirling pattern. Serve immediately.

Banana and Tofu

Ingredients:

2 tablespoons tofu softened

1 banana

Breast milk

Slice the banana and place in a food processor or blender. Add the tofu and a splash of breast milk. Blend until a smooth creamy texture is reached. Chill and serve cold.

Strawberry Nectarine Puree

Ingredients:

3/4 cup strawberries

2 nectarines

Clean and remove tops and centers from the strawberries. Clean, peel, and cut the nectarine into small chunks, removing the seed. In a medium saucepan, steam the strawberries and nectarines for about six minutes. Remove from the heat and place fruit in a food processor or blender. Puree until desired texture is reached. Serve with yogurt or crème fraiche.

Apple Cinnamon Prunes

Ingredients:

1 red apple

3 prunes

Cinnamon

Yogurt (optional)

Preheat the oven to 350 degrees. Wash the apple, cut in half, and remove the core, leaving the peel on. Sprinkle the cinnamon onto the apple. Clean the prunes and stuff the prunes into the center of the two apple halves. Put the halves back together and sprinkle some more cinnamon on the outside. Cover with foil and bake in the oven for 45 minutes. Once cooked, let cool and then cut the apples into chunks. Place in a food processor or blender. Add the prunes and puree until the desired texture is reached. Serve with yogurt.

Other Vegetables

In this section, you'll find recipes for additional vegetables, such as broccoli, cauliflower, green beans, and zucchini. For any of the dishes that create a plain puree, you can enhance the flavor by adding olive oil, butter, and garlic. Cheese also works well with vegetables. Cheddar or Parmesan are two popular choices. Broccoli and asparagus can be served with lemon or mayonnaise for kids who are over one year old. Cauliflower and broccoli are great dipping foods for your older toddler. The trick with most vegetables is to avoid overcooking, as this can give them a slimy texture. Steaming works well and also allows you to maintain the integrity of nutrients. Cooking vegetables in the pan with any roast or chicken also allows them to absorb the flavor of the meat during the cooking process. While these will not be the healthiest vegetables, they will certainly taste good.

Healthy Green Beans

Ingredients:

4 cups fresh cut green beans

1/2 cup of water

Prepare green beans by removing the strings and snipping the ends. Cut or break the green beans in half. Insert a steamer basket into a medium saucepan filled with three inches of water. Add the green beans and steam for 7 - 8 minutes or until tender. Remove the beans and add them to a food processor or blender. Pure until desired texture is achieved. You can add water to thin if necessary.

Cauliflower Puree (6 months)

Ingredients:

4 - 5 cauliflower florets

Water for steaming

Rinse the cauliflower well and trim off any extra leaves. Cut into smaller flowerets. Fill a medium saucepan with three inches of water. Insert the steamer basket. Add the cauliflower florets to the steamer basket. Cover and steam for at least 12 minutes or until tender. Remove cauliflower from the steamer basket and place into a food processor or blender. Puree until desired consistency is reached. Serve with sweet potato.

Breaded Cauliflower

Ingredients:

1½ cups cauliflower cut into florets

1 tablespoon butter

2 tablespoons Parmesan cheese

2 tablespoons bread crumbs

2 tablespoons grated Cheddar cheese

1/4 cup diced tomatoes without the seeds

Preheat the oven to 350 degrees. Fill a medium saucepan with three inches of water. Insert a steamer basket. Add the cauliflower florets to the steamer basket. Cover and steam for about 12 minutes or until tender. In a separate sauté pan, melt the butter, add the bread crumbs and the tomatoes, and sauté until mushy. Take bread crumb and tomato mixture off the heat, add both of the cheeses, and stir until melted. Place the steamed cauliflower florets in a blender or food processor. Add the melted cheese mixture. Puree until desired texture is reached and serve or freeze.

Broccoli Puree (6 months)

Ingredients:

3/4 cups broccoli

Clean the broccoli, cut into florets, and remove any excess leaves. Cut the broccoli into florets and steam until tender. Puree the broccoli to a smooth consistency for babies under 12 months of age.

Sautéed Broccoli Puree

Ingredients:

6 broccoli florets

1/4 cup breadcrumbs

2 tablespoons Parmesan cheese

Olive oil

Preheat oven to 350 degrees. In a small baking dish, add the broccoli florets, and drizzle with olive oil. Cover with cheese and breadcrumbs and mix well. Place in the oven and bake for 15 - 20 minutes. Serve as is or puree to desired texture. This broccoli goes well with chicken or fish dishes.

Sautéed Broccoli

Ingredients:

6-7 broccoli florets

1 tablespoon butter

1/4 teaspoon minced garlic

1 tablespoon grated Parmesan cheese

Water

Heat a sauté pan to medium, add ½ of the butter and garlic, then sauté. Add the broccoli and then add the rest of the butter. Continue to sauté until the broccolis tender. Sprinkle the Parmesan cheese on top. Pour this mix into a blender or food processor. Add a tablespoon of water. Puree until desired texture is reached.

Potato and Zucchini

Ingredients:

3/4 cup cubed zucchini

3/4 cup cubed potato

1/3 cup water

Olive oil

Salt

Wash, peel and cube potatoes and put to boil. Peel the zucchini and cut into cubes. Place the zucchini in a sauté pan with a little olive oil. Add a dash of salt, cover and cook on low heat until the zucchini has softened. Place the cooked potatoes and the zucchini into a blender or food processor, add water and puree until desired texture is reached. Serve with a dollop of sour cream or Cottage cheese.

Roasted Carrots

Ingredients:

2 carrots

Olive oil

Dash of salt and pepper

Maple syrup (optional)

Preheat oven to 400 degrees. Peel, clean, and cut the carrot into thin stick-like pieces (think size and shape of French fries). Place in a medium bowl and drizzle with olive oil. Add just a dash of salt and pepper. Place the carrot sticks on a baking sheet and cook in the oven for 18 to 20 minutes. Coat with maple syrup (optional).

Zucchini Puree

Ingredients:

2 medium zucchinis

Fill a medium sauce pan with three inches of water and then insert a steamer basket. Place on the stove on high and bring water to a boil. Peel, rinse, and cut zucchinis into cubes, then place these cubes in the steamer basket. Steam for about 6 to 8 minutes or until tender. Place cooked zucchinis in a food processor or blender, add breast milk and puree to desired texture.

Broccoli with Cheese Sauce

Ingredients:

5 broccoli florets

5 cauliflower florets

1 tablespoon butter

1 cup milk

5 tablespoons Cheddar cheese

1 tablespoon flour

Clean the broccoli and cauliflower and remove excess leaves. Break into small bite size florets. Place in a steamer basket in a medium saucepan filled with three inches of water. Steam the veggies for 5 -8 minutes or until tender. In a small saucepan, melt butter over low heat. Add the flour and mix well. Slowly add the milk and mix well. Add the cheese and keep stirring until it is melted. You can serve the veggies as is for older kids and allow them to dip in the cheese sauce. For younger kids, puree until smooth and then mix in the cheese sauce.

Parmesan Asparagus Puree

Ingredients:

5 asparagus spears

1 tablespoon butter

1/4 cup Parmesan cheese

Water

Preheat the oven to 400 degrees. Clean the asparagus and break off the ends. Melt the butter. Place in a small baking dish and drizzle the melted butter on top. Grate the cheese over the asparagus and cook in the oven for 20 minutes. Serve as is or puree for younger kids.

Mixed Vegetables

Ingredients:

15 white button mushrooms

1 large sweet potato

1/4 cup finely chopped onion

1 garlic clove minced

1½ teaspoon dried rosemary

1/2 tablespoon olive oil

1/4 cup homemade chicken stock

Preheat your oven to 425 degrees. Clean the mushrooms very well and put them in a medium bowl. Peel the sweet potato, clean well, and cut into slices and add to the bowl with the mushrooms. Add the potatoes, onion and garlic to the bowl. Drizzle the mixture with olive oil. Add salt and pepper and rosemary and mix well. Pour the mixture into a baking dish and cook for 30-35 minutes. Occasionally stir the potatoes in the dish so that they don't stick to the pan.

After the vegetables are cooked, separate out the potatoes, onions, and garlic, then put into a blender or food processor, along with the chicken stock. Puree until a nice smooth texture is reached. You may need to puree this in two parts. Slice the mushrooms and add to the final mixture.

Pasta

Pasta, with all of its sizes and shapes, adds a bit of fun and adventure to any meal. One way to sneak a little spinach into your kid's diet is to purchase spinach pasta. It often comes as a fettuccini or a tortellini. In our book of recipes, we suggest using shells or stars to prevent choking. However, you can use other pastas and just chop or puree them very well so that they don't present as a choking hazard.

If you're making a family casserole, set aside some noodles, cheese, and chicken to serve these to your baby either cut into small pieces or pureed, depending on their age. After age two, you can introduce shellfish to your child's diet, and you can add ingredients such as shrimp to your baby's pasta.

Pasta salad is a great way to serve vegetables, such as corn, peas and carrots, as this makes a great side dish that can be served over a couple of days. Pasta is easy to cook and usually takes about ten minutes for the water to boil and anywhere from ten to twelve minutes to cook the pasta. Check to make sure the pasta is soft enough for your toddler to chew.

It helps to have a big cooking pot with a built in strainer, as this prevents noodles from sticking to the bottom of your pot. Pasta is one of those dishes that you can experiment with to see what you like. One of our favorites is pasta with broccoli, tomatoes, and garlic, cooked in olive oil. This is a very simple and low-cost meal to prepare.

Pasta and Carrots

Ingredients:

1 cup cooked quinoa

1/5 cup steamed carrots

Parmesan cheese

Breast milk

Cook the quinoa as per package instructions. Peel, clean, and cut the carrots into wheels. Mix the pasta, carrots, and cheese. Serve as is or puree to desired texture, adding breast milk as needed.

Lasagna Baby

Ingredients:

1 lasagna noodle, cooked and cut into small squares

1/4 cup Cottage cheese

1/4 shredded Cheddar cheese

1/4 pound ground beef

1/2 cup tomato sauce

1/2 teaspoon olive oil

1 teaspoon minced onion

1/2 clove of garlic minced

1/2 teaspoon basil

Start by cooking the lasagna noodle and set aside. While this is cooking, sauté olive oil, onion, garlic, and the ground beef in a pan over medium heat. Once the meat is thoroughly cooked, add the tomato sauce, basil, and a dash of salt and pepper. Serve the cut up noodles, meat sauce, Cottage cheese, and Cheddar cheese together. You can also puree the ingredients if preferred. This will make at least enough for two or three meals. Refrigerate or freeze any remaining food.

Baby Pasta and Meat Sauce (Over one year old)

Ingredients:

2 cups small pasta shells

1/4 pound lean ground beef

16 ounces of tomato puree

1/4 teaspoon dried basil

1/2 teaspoon olive oil

1/4 teaspoon minced onion

1/4 teaspoon minced garlic

Salt and pepper to taste

Parmesan cheese

In a medium sauce pan, sauté the onions, garlic, and ground beef in olive oil until meat is completely cooked. Add the tomato puree and reduce heat to medium. Add the additional spices, bring the mixture to a boil, and let simmer for 10 minutes. When the pasta is cooked, drain and rinse. Pour the sauce over the pasta and serve as is or puree until desired texture is reached. You can top with Parmesan cheese.

Baby Fettuccini

Ingredients:

1 cup of fettuccini noodles broken into small pieces

2 tablespoons butter

1 tablespoon flour

1/4 cup Parmesan cheese

1/4 cup Romano cheese

1/2 cup milk

Fill a medium sauce pan two thirds full of water, add salt, and bring to a boil. Add shells and cook as per pasta instructions. In another saucepan, melt the butter and stir in the flour. Add the cheese and milk, then stir until the mixture becomes creamy. Pour over cooked and drained pasta and either serve as is or puree to desired texture. You can add peas, ham, or cooked chicken to this dish.

Pasta with Tomatoes and Broccoli

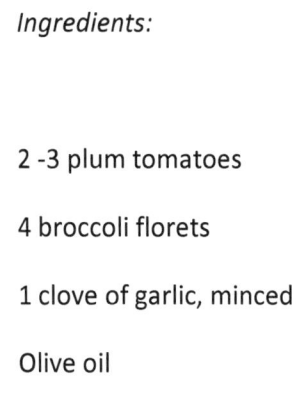

Ingredients:

2 -3 plum tomatoes

4 broccoli florets

1 clove of garlic, minced

Olive oil

1/2 cup of pasta

Fill a large pot two-thirds full of water. Add salt and a splash of olive oil. Bring to a boil on high. Once boiling, add pasta and cook as per the instructions on the package.

Remove the skin from the tomatoes. You can do this by dropping them in the boiling water and then quickly dipping them in cold water. When pasta is halfway done, add the broccoli to the boiling water, and let it cook the remainder of the time.

 Heat a sauté pan and add the olive oil to coat the bottom of the pan. Add the garlic and sauté for a few seconds. Add the tomatoes and continue to stir until the tomatoes get mushy. This takes less than five minutes. When the pasta is done, mix it all together. You can add a dash of salt and pepper to taste. Serve as is or puree to a lighter texture, depending on your child's age.

Pasta with Zucchini

Ingredients:

1 package fettuccini pasta

1 zucchini, peeled and chopped into quarters

1½ tablespoon olive oil

2 cloves garlic, minced

Salt and pepper to taste

1/2 teaspoon basil

Parmesan cheese

Fill a large pot two-thirds full of water. Bring to a boil. Add a dash of salt and olive oil. Prepare zucchini by peeling, cleaning, and cutting into cubes. Preheat a medium to large sauté pan on medium heat. Add the olive oil and minced garlic, stir for about 30 seconds. Add the zucchini, basil, salt, and pepper - continue to sauté until the zucchini is softened. Add the Parmesan cheese. Puree until a smooth texture is reached.

Fish

As moms, we know the importance of fish. You can introduce fish into your baby's diet at seven months of age. Salmon, sole, and cod are good fish to start out with for feeding your baby. Whatever fish that you choose, you want to ensure that it is free of bones, as well as being very fresh. This is why cod tends to be a preferred choice.

Try introducing one fish at a time so that you can watch for any allergic reactions. Wait four days before introducing another type of fish. Being that fish ranges in freshness and smell, ensure that whatever fish you choose to serve is very fresh without any strong or pungent odor. You should learn to recognize between normal fish smell and bad fish smell. You don't want your baby to make a negative association with fish due to it being too smelly or having a fishy taste.

Wait until your baby is about two years old before introducing shellfish due to the risk of allergies.

Fish has earned the nickname of "brain food" due to being a great source of protein, vitamins, and minerals. Salmon could be named the king of fish in the nutrition world, as it contains high stores of omega-3s, and vitamins A and D, which aid in the absorption of calcium, important for the development of healthy teeth and bones.

Fish can be cooked by grilling, baking, steaming, or poaching. Avoid frying the fish, as this is harder for babies to digest. If baking fish, add a little liquid to keep the fish from drying out. Water, milk, breast milk, or lemon (for kids over one year of age) can be used for this purpose. When grilling fish, you can baste it with mayonnaise, which helps seal in juices and flavor. Another option for basting is olive oil, which keeps the fish from sticking to the grill. You can mix the fish with potatoes, rice, broccoli, and carrots.

I've picked these recipes because I have found that they are nutritious and the kids will eat them! When we see the smiles on our children's faces, we know we have made a good choice in foods. Fish is a food that should be introduced at a young age because when a child has fish regularly in their diet, they will eat it as an adult, helping to ensure lifelong health.

Grilled Salmon

Ingredients:

Salmon

Salt and pepper

Olive oil or mayonnaise

Alternative marinade

2 tablespoons soy sauce

5 tablespoons olive oil

1/2 teaspoon mince garlic

1½ tablespoon Dijon mustard

Pre-heat grill. If you're using coals, they should be red hot. However, no flames should be present. Brush the salmon with either olive oil or mayonnaise prior to placing on the grill. Mayonnaise actually helps seal in the juice and flavor of the fish. Sprinkle the fish with a little salt and pepper. If preparing for yourself at the same time, you may want to go heavier on the pepper, as this flavor matches nicely with the salmon. You can also use the alternative marinade listed above. However, since the soy sauce is very salty, you might want to hold off on using this for your baby. Cook the salmon for about four minutes on each side. Remove immediately after this time and serve. (Salmon cooks very fast so if you're planning on using a side dish, it's best to have this prepared prior to beginning to cook the salmon.)

Cream of Cod

Ingredients:

1 fillet of cod

1 tablespoon milk (breast milk may also be used)

1/2 tablespoon melted butter

1 cube of pea puree

I cube of mashed potatoes

Bake the cod in the oven at 350 degrees for about 20 minutes. You'll know that the cod is done when pieces easily flake off. If the mashed potatoes and peas are frozen, defrost prior to cooking the fish. Place the defrosted potatoes, pea puree, fish, milk, and butter in a blender or food processor, then puree to the desired texture. If the mixture seems dry, add a dash more milk.

Cod Casserole

Ingredients:

1 fillet of Atlantic cod

3/4 cup steamed carrots

1/2 cup mild Cheddar cheese

3/4 cup rice or pasta

1 teaspoon lemon juice

1½ teaspoon butter

Pre-heat oven to 350 degrees. Prepare pasta and rice as per package instructions. Cut up the carrots into small bite size pieces. Five minutes before the rice or pasta is done cooking, add the carrots to the pot for steaming.

While the rice is cooking, place fish in a baking dish. Add the lemon juice and coat or dab the fish with the cheese and butter. Cover the fish and place in pre-heated oven. Cook for 20 minutes. The fish is done when pieces flake off easily.

    Combine the cooked fish with the rice or pasta mixture in a blender or food processor. Puree until desired texture is reached. Serve immediately. For older toddlers who can chew, you can complete all of the steps listed; however, forego the puree process.

Salmon with Dill

Ingredients:

Salmon

1½ tablespoon flour

1/4 cup milk or breast milk

1½ tablespoons butter

1/2 teaspoon lemon (for younger kids use water)

1/2 tablespoon finely chopped dill

Check the salmon for bones. Steam the salmon about 10 minutes for each inch of thickness. Set the fish aside and begin to prepare the dill sauce. In a skillet, melt the butter and add the flour to the melted butter. Add the milk and mix until thoroughly combined. Add the lemon juice until the mixture looks like a smooth sauce. Cook on medium for one minute, constantly stirring, then add the dill and cook for another two minutes. Use a fork to mash the fish into the sauce. Serve with rice or potatoes.

Tomato and Basil Cod

Ingredients:

Fillet of cod

1 tablespoon olive oil

1 clove of garlic finely minced

1½ teaspoon fresh basil, chopped finely

1/2 sweet red pepper

1 cup crushed fresh tomatoes

Prepare fish for steaming by cutting into large chunks and removing the bones. Steam fish in a steamer pot until cooked. It will be white all the way through. Puree the garlic, red pepper, basil, and tomatoes in a blender or food processor until smooth.

Add the olive oil to a skillet and put on stove at a medium temperature. Add the pepper mixture to the pan and sauté for about five to six minutes. Remove this mixture from the heat, add the steamed fish to this mixture, and mash into the mixture with the back of a fork. Serve with Stella Luna pasta.

Baked Fish with Sweet Potato

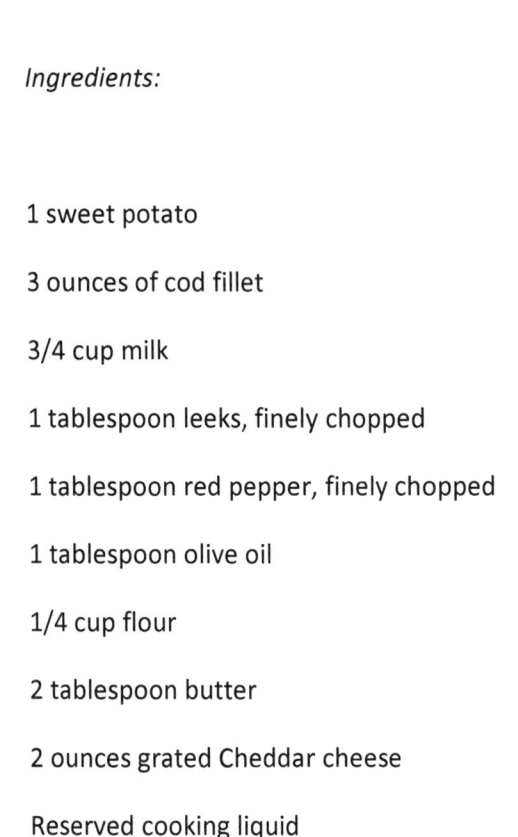

Ingredients:

1 sweet potato

3 ounces of cod fillet

3/4 cup milk

1 tablespoon leeks, finely chopped

1 tablespoon red pepper, finely chopped

1 tablespoon olive oil

1/4 cup flour

2 tablespoon butter

2 ounces grated Cheddar cheese

Reserved cooking liquid

Bake or boil the sweet potato. You will only need half of the potato for this recipe, so plan on refrigerating or freezing the other half. While this is cooking, begin to prepare the fish.

Chop up the leeks and the red peppers to a very fine consistency. In a sauté pan, cook the leeks and red pepper in the olive oil until tender. Put the fish on top of the vegetables and add the milk. Cook the fish for about five minutes and then transfer to another baking dish. Save the liquid from the cooked fish.

Now work on the cheese sauce. Melt the butter in a small sauce pan, add the flour and mix. Once fully combined, add the fish cooking liquid that was set aside. Add most of the cheese, saving a small portion to use as a garnish, and cook until it is completely melted in the oven (about 10 minutes at 250 degrees). Serve with the mashed sweet potato.

Carrot Fish

Ingredients:

1 cup mild fish cooked

1/4 cup of milk

1 tablespoon melted butter

1/4 cup cooked carrots

1/4 cup mashed potatoes

Combine the ingredients in a food processor or blender. Puree until desired texture is reached.

Fish Sticks

Ingredients:

1/2 pound halibut

1 cup small bread crumbs

1 egg, beaten

1 tablespoon water

Preheat the oven to 375 degrees. Cut the fish into 3-inch by 1-inch strips and set aside. Mix the egg and water in a small bowl. Place breadcrumbs in a separate bowl. Dip the fish into the egg mixture and then coat with bread crumbs. Place on a non-stick cooking sheet and repeat until all of the fish has been covered. Place the fish in the oven and cook for about 10 minutes or until the bread crumbs are golden brown. This is a meal that your entire family will like so you may want to multiply this recipe.

Pork

Pork is a great food for your baby, as it is high in vitamins, minerals, and protein. Pork provides your infant with vitamins A, B, C, and niacin. It also contains potassium, phosphorous, magnesium, calcium, sodium, and iron.

Pork is easy to bake in the oven and goes great with many fruits and vegetables, including applesauce, potatoes, and green beans. You can also serve it with rice pilaf or risotto. Pork comes in many different forms including chops, loin roast, and ribs. You can make a loin roast and set some aside to puree for your infant and feed yourself and the rest of your family with the remaining roast. If you opt to make a roast, the leftovers can be used the next day to make tacos or burritos. Thyme and rosemary are good spices to use on pork. However, if you use rosemary, be certain to remove the pieces prior to serving to your infant, as it could scratch their throat.

Creamed Peas and Pork

Ingredients:

4 cups peas, fresh, frozen, or canned as a last resort

1 cup milk

2 tablespoons flour

2 tablespoons butter

Salt and pepper to taste

Pork

In a large sauce pan, melt the butter. Slowly add the flour and mix well. Add the milk stirring continuously to avoid lumps. Add salt, pepper, and other spices as you find appropriate. Cook until sauce begins to thicken. Add peas, stir, and cook until peas are heated through (about 5-7 minutes). Add meat and serve.

Pork, Green Beans, and Potatoes

Ingredients:

1 Russet potato

1/2 cup green beans

6 - 8 ounces of pork

Rosemarie or thyme (optional)

Breast milk

Water

Place the pork in a small baking dish, sprinkle lightly with salt and pepper. You can add the rosemary or thyme if you choose. Add water to cover the bottom of the pan, cover the pan and bake in the oven at 350 for about 30 minutes.

While the pork is cooking, peel the potato and cut into three parts. Place into a medium sauce pan, half filled with water. De-string the green beans and cut off the ends. Place in the same pot with the potatoes and cook for 15 to 20 minutes. Ensure that the potatoes are soft enough to mash. Once cooked, set aside until the pork is done. Cut the cooked pork into smaller pieces and place the pork, the green beans, and the potatoes in a food processor or blender. Puree for about 30 seconds. Make certain that the pork has been completely pureed. Add some breast milk to make the mixture smoother. Serve immediately.

Pork and Sweet Potato

Ingredients:

1 boneless pork chop

1 medium sweet potato

Salt and pepper to taste

Pinch of thyme

Water

Breast milk

Pinch of cinnamon

1 clove of garlic (optional)

Peel the sweet potato and slice into one-inch thick pieces. Fill a medium saucepan with water and add the potato, pork, pinch of thyme, salt, and pepper. Cook until the potato is soft and the meat is cooked through. Drain out the cooking water and discard. Place the meat and the sweet potato slices in a blender or food processor. Add a pinch of cinnamon and breast milk for moisture. Puree until desired texture is reached. Serve immediately.

Red Pepper Pork with Rice

Ingredients:

6 - 8 ounces of pork

8 ounces of fresh cut tomatoes

1½ cup of cooked rice

1/2 sweet red peppers

8 ounces of homemade chicken stock

1/2 small brown onions

1/2 teaspoon ground coriander

1 clove of garlic

1 dash of cumin

1 tablespoon olive oil

Bake pork in the oven for 30 minutes at 350 degrees. Take the pork out of the oven and cut into very small pieces and set aside. Dice the onion and red pepper to a fine texture. Heat the olive oil in a sauté pan, add the onion, garlic, and peppers. Cook until softened. Add the coriander and cumin, stirring the mixture until smooth. Add the crushed tomatoes and the chicken stock - cook for another five minutes on medium heat. Puree the pork sauce and serve it with cooked rice.

Pork in Apricot Sauce

Ingredients:

1 red apple

1/2 medium brown onion

2 - 3 apricots

8 -10 ounces of pork

1½ teaspoon olive oil

1 cup chicken stock

Mince the onion, apple, and apricots into very small fine bits. Cut the pork into bite size pieces and set aside. Heat a sauté pan to medium and add the olive oil. Begin by sautéing the onion, then add the apricot, apple, and pieces of pork. Cook for about two to three minutes, stirring frequently. Add the chicken stock, bring to a boil, and let stand for 15 to 20 minutes or until the meat is cooked through. Serve with mashed potato or sweet potato.

Pork Casserole

Ingredients:

2 boneless pork chops

1 carrot

1 parsnip

1 tablespoon butter

1 teaspoon dried rosemary

1 tablespoon flour

2 tablespoons diced brown onion

1 Russet potato, cut into cubes

2 cups chicken stock

Heat the sauté pan on medium heat and add the butter. Once melted, brown the pork chops on each side, then place the cooked chops in a medium baking dish, leaving the butter in the sauté pan. Now add the carrot, parsnip, and rosemary to the pan, sauté for about one minute. Pour the cooked vegetables on top of the pork in the baking dish. Using a small sauce pan, slowly whisk the flour into the chicken stock. Bring to a boil and then pour this sauce over the pork chops and vegetables. Cover and cook in the oven at 300 degrees for about one hour.

Maui Pork

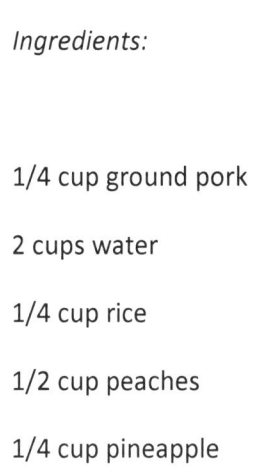

Ingredients:

1/4 cup ground pork

2 cups water

1/4 cup rice

1/2 cup peaches

1/4 cup pineapple

In a medium sauce pan, boil pork and one cup water, then simmer for two minutes. Drain the water and set pork aside. Add the rest of the water, rice, peaches, and pineapples to the meat mixture. Cook on low for 20 minutes. Add the mix to a blender or food processor, then puree until desired texture is reached.

Beef

As you look through our recipes for your baby, you'll see plenty of dishes made with chicken and pork. We have also included a few here using beef. Overall, it seems the best way to prepare beef for your child is by preparing a roast, steak, or burger for the family and setting some aside for your baby. If using steak or roast, make certain that you either puree the meat prior to serving or cut it into very small pieces.

Your baby will like the flavor and probably want to chew on the beef due to the interesting texture. Try not to give big pieces of fat or gristle, as this could present a choking hazard. You can tenderize meat by either pounding with a mallet or marinating overnight. Do not overcook meat, as it will get too dry. A steak needs to cook about six minutes on each side and a roast needs to cook about 30 minutes per pound at 350 degrees. For the perfect tri-tip, preheat your oven to 450 and cook the tri-tip in the oven for 20 to 30 minutes. Then, lower the heat to 350 degrees and cook for about 10 to 20 minutes more, checking the center for preferred doneness.

Hearty Beef Stew

Ingredients:

2 cups of cut potatoes

1 large pinch dried paprika

1 dessert spoon flour

10.5 ounces (about 300 g) beef rump steak

1/2 sweet red paprika

1/2 medium sized onion

2 carrots

2 cups homemade chicken stock

1 garlic clove

5 ounces (about 140g) prunes

A pinch of dried coriander

Heat a frying pan and slightly brown meat, then set aside. Add the bell pepper, garlic, and onions to the pan, then sauté until the onions are soft. Add the flour and meat into the pan and stir until well mixed. Add the prunes, carrots, spices, and finally pour in the chicken stock. Bring the mixture to a boil and then turn the heat to low to medium. Cook for about one hour or until soft and tender.

Creamed Peas and Beef

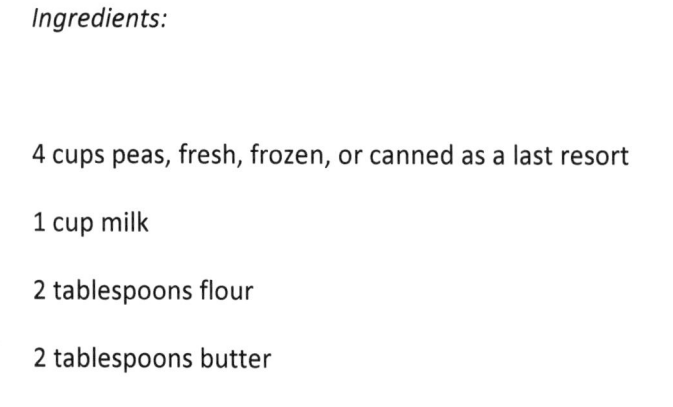

Ingredients:

4 cups peas, fresh, frozen, or canned as a last resort

1 cup milk

2 tablespoons flour

2 tablespoons butter

Salt and pepper to taste

Pieces beef

In a large sauce pan, melt the butter. Slowly add the flour and mix well. Add the milk, stirring continuously to avoid lumps. Add salt, pepper, and other spices as you find appropriate. Cook until sauce begins to thicken. Add peas, stir and cook until peas are heated through (about 5-7 minutes). Add meat.

Beef with Carrots and Potatoes

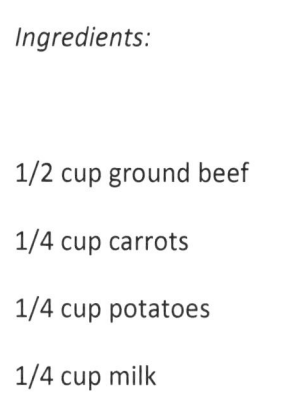

Ingredients:

1/2 cup ground beef

1/4 cup carrots

1/4 cup potatoes

1/4 cup milk

Clean, peel, and chop carrots. Peel, clean, and cut potato into three parts. In a sauté pan, cook the ground beef until brown on all sides. In a medium sauce pan, cook one small potato for 20 minutes. Add cut carrots and cook for another five minutes. Drain the water and place the milk, potatoes, and carrots into a food processor or blender. Puree until desired texture is reached. Serve with the cooked ground beef or add the beef into the puree.

Yummy Meat Sauce

Ingredients:

2 cups zucchini

1/2 pound ground beef

1/2 teaspoon olive oil

1 cup homemade chicken stock

1 stick of celery, finely chopped

1/2 cup chopped onion

2 tomatoes

1 clove of garlic

1/2 teaspoon basil

1 tablespoon tomato puree

Cut the tomatoes into small chunks and puree in the blender or food processor. Add the garlic and the onion. In a medium sauce pan, add the olive oil and sauté the celery and the zucchini for two minutes. Add the ground beef and cook until completely brown on all sides. Pour the tomato mixture into the sauce pan, add the chicken stock, tomato puree, and basil, and then cook for 5 - 10 minutes on medium heat. Serve with pasta or rice as is or puree to desired texture. This makes enough to feed your entire family.

Meatballs

Ingredients:

1 pound ground beef

1/2 tablespoons bread crumbs

1 carrot, peeled and grated

Olive oil

1/2 teaspoon basil salt and pepper to taste

Preheat oven to 350 degrees. Lightly grease a cookie sheet with olive oil. In a medium bowl, mix all of the ingredients together. Form one-inch balls out of the meat mixture and place each meatball on a cookie sheet. Once all of the meatballs are made, place in the oven and cook for 25 minutes. Serve with rice, pasta, and marinara sauce.

Meat Loaf (Over one year)

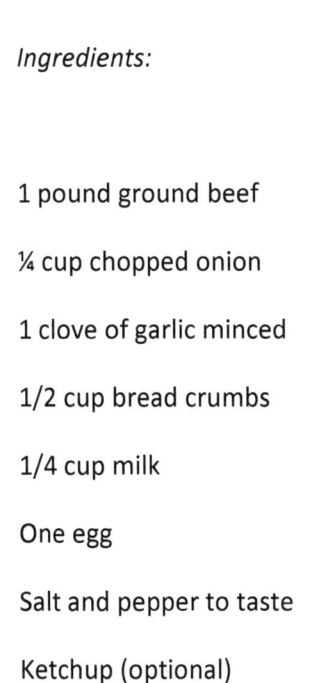

Ingredients:

1 pound ground beef

¼ cup chopped onion

1 clove of garlic minced

1/2 cup bread crumbs

1/4 cup milk

One egg

Salt and pepper to taste

Ketchup (optional)

Preheat oven to 350 degrees. Put all of the ingredients, except the ketchup in a bowl and mix together very well. Take the mixture out of the bowl and place it in a medium baking pan. Form into a rectangular loaf. Cover top of formed meatloaf with ketchup. You can leave a portion without ketchup for your baby. Serve with mashed potatoes as is or puree to desired texture.

Baked Beans

Ingredients:

1 cup dried beans

1/2 teaspoon onion, chopped finely

1½ cup crushed canned tomatoes

2 tablespoons olive oil or vegetable oil

Boil the beans until cooked (keep adding water until the beans are cooked). Heat a frying pan on medium and sauté the onions in the oil. Add the tomatoes and cook for 3 - 4 minutes. Combine the tomato sauce with the beans and cook for a further 5 to 10 minutes, adding a bit more water if needed. Serve with desired cut of beef.

Potatoes

Potatoes are a great side dish or main course that can be served in a number of ways. For babies, a simple mash or puree works quite well and you can make this with russet potatoes, red potatoes, or sweet potatoes. As your infant gets older, you can cut the potatoes into shoestring slices or quarters and drizzle with olive oil, salt, and pepper - baking them in the oven.

For baked russet potatoes, add cheese, sour cream, broccoli, and bacon and serve as a meal. Scalloped potatoes are fairly easy to make by slicing the potatoes thin and layering them in a greased baking dish with butter, cheese, salt, pepper, and adding a little milk. This mixture is baked for about 45 minutes. Breakfast potatoes are a great side dish to serve with eggs.

Potatoes are one of those foods that can be served with every dinner. I never paid quite so much attention to potatoes before until I noticed that my girlfriend had one with every dinner. They're a simple food that offers great variety and can be enjoyed with every meal.

White Potato Puree

Ingredients:

2 medium Russet potatoes

Wash, peel, and cut potatoes into three parts. Boil potatoes for 25 minutes or until tender. Drain the water and place the cooked potatoes in a bowl. Use a potato masher to mash the potatoes. Add either breast milk or a teaspoon of butter to a smooth texture if desired.

Roasted Red Potatoes

Ingredients:

8 -10 small red potatoes

Olive oil

Dash of salt and pepper

Preheat oven to 400 degrees. Peel (optional), clean the potatoes, and cut in half. Place in a medium bowl and drizzle with olive oil. Add just a dash of salt and pepper. Place the potatoes on a baking sheet and cook in the oven for 25 to 30 minutes.

Mashed Potatoes with Spinach

Ingredients:

2 Russet potatoes

1/2 cup fresh green spinach

1/2 cup yogurt

Wash, clean, and set aside the spinach. Clean, peel, and cut potatoes into three parts. Place the potatoes in a medium sauce pan, two-thirds full of water. Place on high heat and bring to a boil. Cook for about 25 minutes or until tender. Prior to draining potatoes, drop the spinach in for about 20 seconds. Remove spinach and set aside. Drain potatoes, place them in a medium bowl, and use a potato masher to mash. Add the spinach and yogurt, mix in well. Serve with chicken, fish, or beef.

Potatoes and Cauliflower

Ingredients:

1 large Russet potato

2 - 3 cleaned cauliflower florets

3 tablespoons butter

2 tablespoons sour cream

Peel, clean, and cut potato into three parts. Put the potatoes in a medium sauce pan two-thirds full of water and bring to a boil. Cook for 15 minutes and add the cauliflower florets. Cook for another 10 minutes or until the cauliflower and the potatoes are tender. Drain the potatoes and cauliflower, then place in a medium bowl. Add the butter and sour cream - mix with an electric mixer. Make certain that the cauliflower is in small enough pieces to avoid choking. Serve immediately.

Scalloped Potatoes

Ingredients:

2 - 3 Russet potatoes

1 block of Swiss cheese

1 clove of garlic

1/2 stick of butter

1/2 cup of milk

Salt and pepper

Preheat oven to 450 degrees. Peel, clean, and thinly slice potatoes and place them in a large bowl with water and a dash of salt. Prepare a medium baking dish by greasing with butter and then rubbing the dish with a sliced, open clove of garlic. Take some of the potatoes, pat them dry on a paper towel, and then make a layer of the slices on the bottom of the pan. Cut small chips of butter and sprinkle these on top of the potato layer. Grate the cheese and sprinkle over the butter. Add some salt and pepper.

Repeat above steps until all of the potatoes have been layered. It should make about three layers. Pour the milk around the edges of the baking dish. Place the dish in the oven and bake for 45 minutes. Puree a portion and serve the rest to your family. You can substitute Cheddar cheese for the Swiss for a slightly different flavor. Give yourself time to make this dish, as the combined prep time and cook time ends up being at least 1½ hours.

Cheese

Cheese is a great source of protein, calcium, and contains vitamins A and B. Cheese is a great addition to many meals and can be mixed into potatoes or rice, used as a sauce for vegetables, added to salads or shredded, and eaten as a finger food.

Mozzarella string cheese is a simple, healthy snack that you can give your toddler. As you purchase cheese for your baby, it's important to ensure that it's pasteurized, as this is less likely to be infected with the bacteria called Listeria. While cheeses, such as Brie, Camembert, and Bleu Cheese are yummy, they are not the best option for your baby, as they are not made from pasteurized milk.

Some popular cheeses include Cheddar, Monterey Jack, Parmesan, Romano, Ricotta, Cottage cheese, and Cream cheese. Remember that processed cheeses may contain additives and preservatives, which are not healthy. You might want to avoid these products. Check the labels on the cheese products that you purchase to ensure that they are made with pasteurized milk.

Cheesy Baked Potato

Ingredients:

1 Russet potato

2 tablespoons Cheddar cheese

1 tablespoon butter

1 dollop sour cream (optional)

Preheat oven to 450 degrees. Wash the potato and poke on both sides with a fork. Place potato in the oven and cook for 45 minutes. Cut potato in half lengthwise. Carefully scoop out the potato into a bowl, saving the shell. Add the cheese and butter to the potato. Mix well and scoop the mixture back into the potato skins. Place in the oven at 350 degrees for 10 minutes. Let cool for five minutes and serve. You can top with a dollop of sour of sour cream if you choose.

Mac 'n Cheese

Ingredients:

3/4 cup grated Cheddar cheese

3/4 cup small shell pasta

1/4 cup milk

1 tablespoon flour

1 tablespoon butter

In a medium saucepan, boil the pasta on medium to high heat for 8 minutes. Drain the pasta and set aside. In the same pan, melt the butter. Once it is fully melted, slowly add the flour. Mix well and add the milk. Add the cheese and continue to stir until the cheese melts. You can also use a mixture of cheese, such as Cheddar, Jack, and Mozzarella. Once the cheese melts and is saucy, add the pasta and mix well. Serve as is or puree to the desired texture.

Shells with Parmesan and Butter

Ingredients:

1 - 2 tablespoons Parmesan cheese

1 tablespoon butter

1/2 cup pasta shells

In a medium saucepan, boil the pasta shells on medium to high heat. Cook for eight minutes or until tender. Drain pasta and place in a medium bowl. Add the butter and cheese, mix well. You can serve as is or puree to desired texture.

Cottage Cheese with Peaches

Ingredients:

1 medium sized peach

1/2 cup Cottage cheese

Peel and clean the peach. Cut into very small bite size pieces or puree to desired texture. Mix the fruit with the Cottage cheese. Add a dash of cinnamon if desired. You can substitute avocados, apricots, plums, peaches, or cooked carrots for the peach.

Sliced Cheese and Grapes

Ingredients:

Hard cheese such as Cheddar, Monterey Jack, or Gouda

Crackers, Melba toast or toast

Red or green grapes

Clean the grapes and cut into quarters. You can leave grapes whole for kids over two years of age. Place on a plastic plate. Slice cheese and place on same plate. Add Melba toast, crackers, or cut up pieces of toast. Serve as a snack or appetizer. Your toddler will love this finger food and being able to serve himself.

Cheesy Quesadillas

Ingredients:

1/4 cup grated Cheddar cheese

1 medium tortilla

Preheat a griddle or sauté pan to medium heat. Grate the cheese and sprinkle on the inside surface of the tortilla. Fold the tortilla in half and place in the heated pan. Cook until golden brown on each side. Once cooked, open up the tortilla to allow the cheese to cool prior to serving to avoid burns. Serve with avocados, tomatoes, and sour cream.

Thank you for purchasing our book and reading it!

We hope that you gained a lot of information and insight into making your own wonderful, nutritious, wholesome, and above all, delicious baby food for your little ones. We can't stress how much you and your family will benefit from making your own baby food at home.

It's a wonderful part of being truly a part of your baby's growing up process, you are in charge of everything that goes into your baby's mouth. In today's tough economic times, making your own baby food saves so much money for the average family that it's truly worth doing for you and your family. Sure, making your own baby food takes a little more time, but believe us, it's definitely worth it.

I hope you enjoyed our book and that we were able to make a difference in the well-being and health of your beautiful baby. Thank you and we hope you are blessed with many years of memories to cherish as you raise your family. It's a time that is truly precious.

Please be sure to share the joy of making your own baby food to your friends, family, and co-workers.

Printed in Great Britain
by Amazon.co.uk, Ltd.,
Marston Gate.